PRAI...

...a book that everyone who has ever wondered why he hunts, how to justify killing of game or how to answer those who criticize hunting should read.
Jim Casada

Jones's work is one of the finest examinations ever published of man's role as a hunter.
John McCoy

AND FOR LAST YEAR'S RIVER

Allen Jones knows the West by heart.
William Kittredge

As clean as wind and water and stone...
Rick Bass

Allen Jones's book is full of strengths, not least of which is its furious readability.
Thomas McGuane

The quiet space in which his characters...reside is what carves out a niche for this book that has formerly been occupied only by true literary greats.
Barnes & Noble
Discover Great New Writers Citation

Jones has a way of making the starkest elements, even pain, seem inevitably linked with beauty.
Gretchen Schwartz
Associated Press

Allen Morris Jones's debut is a novel of Wyoming...yet, against this panoramic backdrop, what emerges is a rendering of smaller internal landscapes that are, in their way, no less grand.
The Los Angeles Times Book Review

A Quiet Place of Violence

A Quiet Place *of* Violence

Hunting and Ethics in the
Missouri River Breaks

by

Allen Morris Jones

Montana
2012

Copyright © 1997 by Allen Morris Jones, Inc.

Introduction, Copyright © 2012
by Allen Morris Jones, Inc.

ISBN-13: 978-0-9828601-4-4

Manufactured in the United States of America
10 9 8 7 6 5 4 3

All rights reserved. With the exception of short excerpts used for promotional, review, or academic purposes, no portion of this work may be reproduced or distributed in any print or electronic form without the written permission of the publisher.

Published in the United States by

Bangtail Press
P. O. Box 11262
Bozeman, MT 59719
www.bangtailpress.com

Cover photo by Allen Morris Jones
Back cover photo: Sascha Burkard / Shutterstock

To my brother,
and our father,
and his father:
quiet hunters.

Introduction

Author Italo Calvino believed that writers can be defined by their first book. You carry the definition, he said, for the rest of your life, "trying to confirm it or extend or correct or deny it; but you can never eliminate it."

A Quiet Place of Violence scrolled out of a printer more than seventeen years ago now. In retrospect, it came after an unusual amount of angst and uncertainty. I finished it in the summer of 1994, and was pretty sure that I had written a worthwhile book. But what *kind* of book. An academic thesis? A call to arms? A memoir? I didn't know, and nobody else really did, either. When I submitted it to all the obvious presses, I received all the predictable rejections. But when it was finally published by a small house in Montana, the response (thank god) was warm enough to reassure. In fact, a number of the original publishers came back to me later, asking for paperback rights. I've resisted until now.

Since the first edition, there have been advances in several of the disciplines discussed in this book, particularly anthropology. But largely because I find myself devoted to the prose, to the language itself, I've decided to leave the content much as it was originally published. The central thesis stands unaffected.

For being such a short work, I've found that *A Quiet Place of Violence* has come to take on a place of undue importance in my life. It means a great deal to me that I'm able to share it with you now. All these years later, it still feels like I'm offering up an essential piece of myself.

Allen Morris Jones
Bozeman, Montana
May, 2012

Author's Note

I began this work with a set of ideas that I naively assumed to be new. As I familiarized myself with the issues, however, I found that I had been preceded on a number of fronts.

A modern, philosophical view of hunting was first written in 1942 by the Spanish philosopher José Ortega y Gasset. Titled *Meditations on Hunting,* it is still the best work available for a thorough, thinking view of the act. The concept of treating the natural world as a single, ethical entity was first proposed by Aldo Leopold in 1949. An expansion and explication of Leopold's land ethic has been admirably treated by J. Baird Callicott. The sections on Indian mythology owe a debt to Catherine L. Albanese's *Nature Religion in America.* For those with an interest in anthropology, *Man the Hunter* (Richard B. Lee and Irven de Vore, Editors) is the canonical defense of human predatorial development. Finally, a collection of essays, *The Wilderness Condition* (Max Oehlschlaeger, Editor), provides a superb introduction to a number of the issues touched on in this work. Paul Shepard's essay, "A Post-Historic Primitivism," is especially valuable, and does a good job of condensing down the basic gist of his thought. My treatment of the physical necessity of meat eating and the social benefits of hunting are largely derived from Shepard's work.

This is a book of synthesis. As such, I believe its primary value lies in a newish treatment of previous ideas. So far as I am aware, this is the first attempt to devise a hunting ethic based on the ideas of Ortega and Leopold.

The narrative was derived, with certain large liberties, from actual experiences. I apologize for these changes, however structurally necessary they may have been. I apologize specifically to the friends and family with whom I shared many of the experiences; if I left you out, it's only because I am too close to paint you with any realism or objectivity.

The help and encouragement of my mother and father made this work possible.

> "Do I know nature yet?
> Do I know myself?"
> —Arthur Rimbaud

Part I

Absorption and Reflection

Beginnings

You know that what you're doing, trying to kill an animal, is important and good, but you don't *know*.

You stutter over attempts to describe the experience, rationalizing in the face of a question that you're sure needs no response: It is a given.

I live on a ranch in the Missouri River Breaks of Eastern Montana. There are steel buildings on this ranch and a cabin and grain fields that fold down into rough grazing country. The Breaks themselves are most usually bare across the top but turn rugged in the bottom, choked with pine and juniper. They can be impenetrable. Still, we can't help thinking that these tight ravines are where the largest bucks die of old age. So. Although the grain fields harbor the largest populations of deer, we spend most of our time hunting the rough country. A semiannual glimpse of that buck old enough to have acquired a name, ducking over the horizon, confirms our faith.

Elk are harder. In bow season, when it's legal to hunt them without a drawn permit, herds of them get pushed back and forth as each farmer's hunter gets his turn at them. Sometimes, it's like they don't stay long enough to take a deep breath.

I'm sitting on the porch of our cabin: my first night here after an absence of several months. I'm drinking coffee. It will probably keep me awake until morning, but it's chilly on the porch.

It's so incredibly still here. Except for the days when you start your truck or answer the phone, there's only the wind in the curve of your ear. On the roof of my cabin, an owl's beak scrapes against a small rabbit's skull. Somewhere on the ranch, coyotes grunt into the stomach of their deer. A rifle shot, on cold mornings, is enough to break the air into fragments.

The ranch includes over seven thousand acres of deeded land, with more grazing leased from the Charles M. Russell National Wildlife Refuge. The nearest town is Jordan, fifty miles to the south and east, with a population of five hundred. Topping the rise above the cabin, coming home at night, the only light in the entire world comes from the mining operation at Zortman, sixty miles to the north across Fort Peck Lake.

I've come here in late summer to begin exploring. This is the country for explorations. It has a history in the western imagination of the unknown and the dark, of blank places on maps and sandstone obelisks. This will be an exploration of self—an inscribed Mercator projection of motivation and will and of the larger, western mind of which I am a part. Why am I hunting? Indeed.

What justification or, perhaps, what ethics, could rationalize any pursuit that ends in such noise and blood and inevitable sense of loss? Why kill another animal if you don't have to?

The question Why has worried humans since, presumably, we began ceremonial burials seventy thousand years ago. How has not been a problem. Or perhaps only a problem to be contained by succeeding generations. How has given us air conditioning and fax machines. Why has given us fits.

This particular Why, I feel, I sense, has the capacity to expose the entire system of our western approach to nature. Hunting is the taproot consideration, the anchoring thread that has lately been taking the brunt of a culture's changing attitudes. It has been involved with 99 percent of human evolution and has been one of the principal factors in shaping our relationship toward nature.

The question *why* has driven me here to spend a fall hunting and thinking, to dig through the layers to the sensed, final conclusion. I know, but I don't *know*.

The genesis for this work lies in two separate experiences. At the age of fourteen, I killed a mountain lion south of Livingston, Montana. He treed on a near vertical slope, and my shot, when it came, pierced the top of his lung and severed the spinal chord, paralyzing his back legs. It was enough to knock him from the tree but not enough to kill him. He swatted at the dogs as he slid down the slope, shattering his claws against the shale. I approached him from the front for the final shot, and from four or five feet away he looked up at me, half his face bloody, half white with snow, the eyes red. He snarled...and memory suspends him there.

This arrested piece of energy has stayed with me; has, in some ways, haunted me.

The second incident involved a Dall sheep killed when I was eighteen. After ten days and over 120 miles of backpack hunting, I sat alone with the dead sheep, holding my skinning knife. Snow was falling and his legs and neck were stiffening in the cold. His eyes were glazing. Depth was replacing reflection. Was this right? I stroked his neck down to its base, to the point of my final shot, and my hand came away bloody. What a thing I had just done. Was it an accomplishment or an aberration?

How had given me a trigger to pull. *Why* would force me to consider whether I should have pulled the trigger at all.

Both experiences contain some commonalities that, I think, give reason for their strength. I was young, and my opinions were being formed by images and emotions rather than disciplined thought. Both kills came after extremes of physical exertion when the mind is peculiarly susceptible to strong impressions (we had followed the lion to treeline three times over fourteen hours). But more importantly, each incident contained a moment of communion with the animal, when it was perceived not as an object, perhaps not as a subject, but as something beyond that dichotomy. In both cases, it was a meeting of eyes and flesh.

I have been led here.

*F*rom *my seat on the porch, the blackness in the east seems to be graying, though this may be my imagination.*

There's a dull ache at the back of my eyes that goes away when I blink.

Something's walking up from the pond. It steps out of the water and shakes itself and starts moving toward me, rustling through the grass. It radiates noise like a pulsing of wind, except there is no wind.

Of course, wind by itself is the essence of silence. It's only when it's confronted by trees or bluffs or the side of a cabin that it whispers and howls. I would like to turn against the wind, to confront full force those issues which hunters know instinctively but which antihunters attack with the strength of western rationality. I want to explore the truths and misconceptions of each position and come to a final conclusion, raising up into the wind to take my first real breath.

Process

*I*t's late summer, only a few days into August, and the mosquitoes are swarming. It's been a particularly wet season, and the mosquitoes have taken advantage of it to multiply like amoebas. A short walk through the yard brings them swarming up around my head. Yesterday afternoon I stopped and counted nearly fifty on the legs of my jeans. That's something natural selection hasn't taught them to deal with, loose fabric hanging away from flesh. But my arms have acquired, between them, nearly twenty bites. They love all this soft, pink flesh served up through a cotton shirt.

I'm sitting on a sandstone outcropping above Lost Creek, glassing down into it for movement. Bow season isn't for another six weeks, but I've already begun scouting. Strings need to be reattached. You lose a sense of propriety when you've been away too long, in the same way that hermits lose their sense of social conduct: blowing their noses into their hands, laughing out of context.

The high points of these drainages have been defined by their ability to resist erosion. A butte is only a butte to the extent that deposits of sandstone and shale rest on top in such a way as to shed the water. They make wonderful places to sit.

The sandstone is grainy and slightly moist under my hand, and when I rub back and forth, specks of the rock come off on my palm. This is one of my favorite spots: a predator's perch.

Local geology insists that the sandstone rubbing off on my palm was deposited during the Cretaceous. Eighty million years ago, this whole place was under an inland sea, catching sand and mud as they ran out of the forming Rocky Mountains.

As a primate I have traceable roots that go back thirty million years.

According to the infinity of the moment, wherein each instant can be split into two more, I have been sitting here forever and will be sitting here forever.

A different type of seeing.

Consider the order of the Breaks. This is what I've been thinking about for the past few days: order.

Plato showed us the importance of adequate definitions. Euclid and Descartes argued for the importance of a solid, incontrovertible base. If the ridgepole is sound, a definition can be strong enough to support an entire *knowing* structure.

We all refer to nature constantly, yet what is it?

We speak of human nature. When we have to go to the bathroom, we say "nature calls." We refer to it as something beyond ourselves. We go into the hills to "get back to nature." Any extravagance that has to do with the body rather than the mind—hot tubs, feather pillows, leather furniture—we call "creature comforts."

Most of us would look at a mountain stream and think of it as purely natural, just as we would look at New York City and say, "Unnatural." Yet we control the amount of water flowing through the stream, we stock the fish, we eliminate certain types of insects in the interests of crop or timber production, we extinguish forest fires. Nature has traditionally been defined as that which stands apart from civilization—yet the boundary has blurred.

My cabin stands just below the upper juncture of two major drainages: Lost Creek and Hay Coulee. From the cabin, Lost Creek is out of sight behind me, but I can look from my porch down into Hay Coulee. The coulee begins as a slice through a hay field, barely enough of a depression to support a few cottonwoods. It turns south a mile or so past the cabin and runs into a larger, forested drainage—Squaw Creek—which in turn empties out into Fort Peck Lake. Lost Creek begins over the hill to the northeast, a much larger drainage that speaks first to space rather than substance, eating into its original, depositional flatness.

Beginnings are such subtle things.

White *movement on a grassy bench on the other side, and my predator's eye is immediately drawn to it. Through the binoculars, the speck becomes a solitary antelope buck running back and forth mindlessly, the tips of his horns low to the ground. I suppose that he's running from mosquitoes. You expect this behavior from Alaskan caribou, but not from Montana antelope. Another* predator has just been added to his list: dual-winged, female, voracious. I lean back on my hands and feel absurdly grateful for my repellent.

Without the binoculars, the antelope immediately drops back to a trembling spot of white, ten times further away than it was three seconds ago.

Unless they're moving, deer and antelope are hard to spot across these wide drainages. Even with binoculars, it's difficult to see antlers. I only know that the antelope across from me now is a buck because of its darker face. You mostly find yourself guessing the sex of the animal based on body movement and size. Elk, being larger and darker, are easier.

This far from the cabin, the drainage belongs entirely to the Wildlife Refuge. As often as I've sat on these rocks, I've never seen another person. To my right—to the north—the drainage opens wide before emptying out into the lake. Because it's been such a wet year, the sun reflects off pieces of water, caught in separate pools in the dry creekbed. To my left, the artery of space clamps off into an abrupt tangle of ponderosa pine and junipers. I'm alone and floating.

A wind picks up from the south, sweeping away the mosquitoes. Rain clouds build to the north. Like any large body of water, the Fort Peck affects weather patterns. Most of our evening weather seems to come from the north, where the day-heated reservoir has pushed the air to a height of condensing coolness. Of course, the moisture has to be there first. In previous years the wind has twisted a number of range fires out of dry thunderstorms. The burnt foliage returns nutrients to the soil, clears old-growth grasses, stimulates the growth of ponderosas by allowing the seeds to germinate, and provides jobs for the government fire fighters that at least one rancher calls parasites.

There is a rumor among the locals (who dislike the ponderosas for eating into their good grazing space) that Indians used to intentionally burn this country at the end of each hunting season. Implicitly, they are saying that the amount of timber here is unnatural. They are more than likely correct. Even if the Atsina and Assiniboine didn't burn it, lightning would have, on an average of every twenty-five years, if the historians are right.

The sun engenders the first growths. I have read that on a clear day the sun can beat the equivalent of 4,500 horsepower units of energy down onto an acre of ground. Alfalfa on this acre can grow to flower, be pollinated by insects, and be eaten by the antelope across the drainage. The antelope's excreta will help fuel the next generation of alfalfa, as will the decomposition of its final body. So that the antelope as a species don't overpopulate and turn the prairie into a desert, there are coyotes, as there were, at one time, wolves. Any predator/prey relationship is exquisitely self-regulating: too many antelope and the coyote population grows in compensation, too many coyotes and the antelope fall back and force the coyote population down. The coyote dies, having lived its life through blood, and is returned to the soil to fuel the next generation of alfalfa.

These relationships are the concern of that branch of science called ecology. More specifically, ecology is interested in the trophic movement of energy within a system: things eating and things being eaten. Energy can be traced from plant to antelope to coyote, with units lost at each level in the acts of running, breeding, and defecating. In a semi-arid climate like the Breaks—in an environment of limited resources—it is in an animal's best interest to minimize the amount of energy used in the struggle for food and reproduction. The more efficiently it can gather and retain energy, the more likely it is to survive. This constant push and pull of energy movement defines the impossibly complex relationships between the animals and their environment. It's a perfect order, but an order that depends upon movement within the system. Ecology is a process of change.

If ecology is a process concerned with *current* relationships within the system, evolution is a process concerned with *past* relationships, and how these have manifested themselves in changes within a species.

Darwin's theory of natural selection states simply that all forms of life developed from earlier, less successful forms due to genetic differences between individuals within a species. An African ungulate evolves a trait of herding (since more eyes mean less danger of surprise), and in order to more successfully utilize the energy of the gazelle, a cat evolves a greater speed (allowing it to depend less on surprise). Toss in a few other variables over a period of fifteen or twenty million years and you have a springbuck and cheetah.

Every aspect of life—bark on trees, color in the pupils, a four-chambered heart—owes its existence to the forces of natural selection. The fact that this is occasionally hard to believe speaks only to our inability to conceive, in any real way, just how *long* natural selection has been operating. Life on earth is at least 3.5 billion years old. For the purposes of human imagination, this is an eternity.

Ecology and evolution are grounded in periods of tranquility marked by occasional eruptions of violence. From this pulse emerges, finally, a perfect balance. In the West, we've been reduced to calling this process, in one of our more vulgar simplifications, "Nature."

But the process continues, regardless of its name. Environments change, and the biomass within any one environment changes with it or grows extinct. Any element of the ecosystem not open to change is selected out until all that's left *is* process.

We must turn from the notion, pounded into us from childhood, that death is an evil. Its value, in the natural world, is in sculpting form and function from a few animated pieces of carbon. There's no order to life which death has not put there.

How many of us think of a robin flying to its nest with a worm in its mouth as a predator? A beautiful flower, the yellow pea, grows here on the south slopes in May. It has evolved its petals and odor as sexual organs, designed to stimulate reproduction. But sex is only necessary to the extent that individuals within the species will die. Predators evolve to kill more efficiently, filling niches left open by their potential prey. The prey evolves to create new niches, new ways of avoiding their predators. The changes finally give rise to peacocks and crocodiles, roses and crabgrass. This is the confusing, perfect order of the process. Death is calling the dance.

Annie Dillard points out that a circle of 136 hydrogen, carbon, oxygen, and nitrogen atoms around a single atom of magnesium is chlorophyll. Replace the atom of magnesium with an atom of iron and you have hemoglobin. The world is within a whisker of having been washed in blood. Six days for creation is poppycock.

And a seventh for rest? Stick your head out the window. Creation is happening on the porch. We're smack in the middle of it. There is no day for rest, no rest at all.

These are patterns, not laws. Laws are unchangeable; patterns, by their nature, move. We need to believe in a perfect order that is free to move into another, equally-perfect order. The essence of nature is not in any one animal, any one plant, any one rainstorm, but in the relationship of the animal, the plant, and the rainstorm. Nature must be seen in terms of systems rather than laws.

Patterns are inclusive: within a pattern everything finds a place within the larger construct. Laws are exclusive: the namer of the law has tried to achieve control through naming. In a pattern, exclusions are lost, and every boundary becomes a center.

Storm clouds are boiling up from the north in a dark, threatening bruise; thunder somewhere behind them. I stand up to leave. When this ground has any amount of moisture at all, it turns into "gumbo," a word that manages to suggest gum and dumb. There is some sand and silt, but the soil is mostly a mixture of clays. You drive on it, and pretty soon you find the road sticking to your tires—all of it. You walk on it, and within a few steps you're walking on circular mounds of clay and grass. You kick it off your feet and within twenty steps the tendons behind your knees are feeling the stress.

My truck's a quarter mile or so back from the edge, and as I walk, I begin to breath a little harder. Even the age of the oxygen atoms cycling through my lungs is enough to confuse. Ahhh, there was a molecule that had passed through Socrates's lungs. Ahhh, Jesus's. Ahhh, a doe and fawn, hiding down in the ravine. Ahhh, the red-tailed hawk perched on the pine tree at the top of the hill.

I drive back through my own tracks in the grass. Before I'm within a mile of the cabin, a shot of thunder and lightning arrive together. Rain follows with a pounding strength that, if it were to last more than a few minutes, would fray the ground out from under the tires of my truck.

Definitions are necessary. This is *my* definition: Nature is a process. Predation and parasitism, mutualism and reciprocity...everything natural moves in a changing order. New York City, in that it lies outside the process, is mostly unnatural. The mountain stream is *more* natural, although given our manipulation, is not *perfectly* natural.

We have been produced by the process even while trying to step away from it. We're the first animal able to manipulate the system in such a way that we can feel that the laws of ecology and evolution, for the moment, no longer apply to us.

Within the system, wherein each part should be a reflection of every other part, we have found some advantage to absorption. We are, in this way, a new kind of parasite. Fifty mosquitoes on my pants legs, ticks on my head, mice under my dresser...angels by any measure of parasites that would also include us, their hosts. In the past ten thousand years we've grown away from our original role to become unreciprocating, unsymbiotic, and unappreciative.

How many things interact with a Goodyear tire? What nests in an exhaust pipe? What eats the body of an old truck?

One of the more reliable measures of the health and

stability of an ecosystem lies in the variety and number of its members. The healthiest ecosystems sustain the most complex relationships. New York, Los Angeles, Houston—these are aberrations in the simplicity of their systems, containing as members only *Homo sapiens sapiens* and our parasites: rats, cockroaches, pigeons.

We've got quite a lot of damned gall, actually, calling ourselves "Wise, *Wise* Man."

Ironically, the systems we've so proudly created are separated only for the moment, even if we tend to approach them as eternal. The *fact* of our inevitable connection to nature cannot be denied. It is our *awareness* of this connection, or lack of it, that is the area of concern. We've separated ourselves away from the process to such an extent that the abuse and simplification of a system is now accepted as inevitable and normal. Given time, of course, the tire will dry and crumble, the concrete will split, the buildings will fall. But we've forgotten it.

Ultimately, we cannot be separated from the process that produced us. But here's the danger: We *think* we can. We think we *are*.

By *the time I reach the cabin and turn off the truck, the rain has stopped. The only sound, after the tick of the cooling engine, comes from water rolling off the roof.*

It can be so quiet here. It's like you've caught the Breaks between breaths. You find yourself waiting with them for the next great thing. I move to the porch and lean against a post, watching. It would seem impossible, in this silence, that the world could have been created by violence and death. But the violence has been caught between breaths as well. It's now thought that natural selection doesn't occur at a steady, gradual rate, as Darwin believed, but as a series of punctuated eruptions. A species radically changes in a cosmic moment, and then is left to rest through a period of stability.

The blood of violence would seem to be in opposition to the skin of quiet folding around me now, but they are responsible for each other. We speak, and our words must be preceded by, and followed by, silence.

History

The rain began again yesterday evening and ended just a few hours ago. The reservoir below the house has risen two or three feet in twenty-four hours, the few hundred acres of clay above the house shedding water like goose feathers. There are no constantly-flowing streams in the Breaks, no babbling brooks, just these occasional commas of water created by runoff.

Rapid runoff and erosion are responsible for the Breaks. The potential for such erosion is tremendous, but like evolution it tends to happen in chunks.

The sun came out this afternoon, and the temperature has already risen fifteen or twenty degrees. The clays that had flowed from point to point this morning will, by this time tomorrow, have been baked into a kiln-fired solidity.

If nature is a process, then how do we fit within it?

Rationality has helped displace us from nature through technology, language, and perhaps certain aspects of religion, but these are prosthetics on an essentially sound limb. Rationality can return us as well.

The argument in anthropology called *Man the Hunter* asserts that the primary force behind human evolution has been our role as predators. We are what we are—we walk upright, have large brains, sweat, and use tools—because of our need to hunt more efficiently.

The first undoubted primate was a nine-pound fruit eater that lived thirty million years ago in the Nile River valley. Twenty-five million years and a few intermediate species later, *Australopithecus afarensis* stepped across East Africa. In this same time period, India and Saudi Arabia attached themselves to Europe, the Rocky Mountains slowed their formation, the earth's climatic fluctuations forced the retreat of Africa's tropical forests, and our ancestors began walking on their hind legs.

Gracile *Australopithecus* bled into *Homo habilis* about 2.25 million years ago. *Habilis* was the first to begin fracturing rocks into cutting edges, and he existed *at least* as a meat-eating scavenger. His brain expanded from the 450 cc's found in *Australopithecus* to about 750 cc's (chimpanzees have a capacity of roughly 400 cc's). The parietal and temporal regions of the brain, the centers of sensory intelligence and learning, were part of this growth. More importantly, Broca's area—the seat of language development—first appeared with *habilis*.

Homo erectus showed up in East Africa 1.6 million years ago, a descendant of *habilis*. Fossil evidence shows *erectus* to have been the first undoubted hunter, as well as the first fire user. The brain again expanded, to 1300 cc's, and there were further modifications in the hips and limbs. *Erectus* evolved in tropical Africa, but by 700,000 years ago had followed its prey species into Europe and Asia.

In Europe, *erectus* evolved as an isolated population into *Homo sapiens neanderthalensis*—a species that was within a brow ridge of being *Homo sapiens sapiens*.

Modern humans officially skipped *neanderthalensis* and evolved directly out of *erectus* in the African savanna about 100,000 years ago. We migrated and spread into the Mediterranean basin and the near East about 45,000 years ago, moved into Europe not long after (replacing *neanderthalensis*), migrated to the New World anywhere between 45 and 15,000 years ago, and rediscovered ourselves in 1492 on the ocean blue.

It's easy, on any mountaintop, to confuse yourself with the slow warp and bulge of geology. But how often do we consider the warp and bulge of our own evolution, the environmentally-sponsored mutations that gave me ten fingers, blue eyes, and an understanding of language? In less than six million years, I have risen up off of my knuckles, my suborbital lobe and prominent jaw have receded, my thumb has moved forward into a position of opposition with the fingers, my dentition has grown more delicate, and, most importantly, my brain has tripled its volume.

There is no doubt that *Homo* evolved as a hunter, but has hunting been incidental to our evolutionary success or has it been the essential component?

It's important that although *Homo erectus* is the first of our ancestors to have *certainly* hunted, we *probably* hunted before *erectus*, perhaps even before *Australopithecus*. According to genetic evidence, we share a common ancestor with chimpanzees. Our clades split about six to seven million years ago. And modern chimpanzees (specifically, an Ivory Coast population) have been seen hunting cooperatively. A group of males regularly sets ambushes and drives game toward an apparently pre-chosen hunter. This hunter then shares the meat with as many as twenty other members of the pack.

Reactive arguments have been made that it was our role as gatherers that propelled us into evolutionary stardom. A more intelligent gatherer, the argument goes, is a more efficient gatherer. A gatherer that can walk long distances is more likely to survive in times of drought than one that is designed primarily for short sprints and predator evasions.

In terms of energy budgeting, however, these adaptations benefit the hunter far more than the gatherer.

What are advances in hunting technology if not a more efficient use of energy? I expend less energy by killing an animal with a spear than by running it into a bog and clubbing it to death; less by killing it with a bow and arrow than a spear; less with a rifle than a bow and arrow. We began flaking cutting edges from rocks in order to more efficiently utilize the energy of other species (in butchering as well as killing), and 2.5 million years later I can shoot with a telescopic sight and a rifled barrel.

Hunting *has* to be the parent of technology.

It also seems likely that language owes a debt to hunting. It's a great energy benefit to the hunter to be able to communicate well. *Habilis* was the first to begin developing the brain capacity for language, but it was *erectus* who developed the physical capacity to articulate a wide

A Quiet Place of Violence

variety of sounds. All mammals, except *erectus* and *Homo sapiens*, have a larynx high in the neck, allowing them to breath and swallow at the same time even while limiting the range of possible sounds. The pharyngeal chamber in *erectus* and *sapiens*, however, grew and enlarged above the vocal cords, allowing an almost infinite modification of sounds.

The coincidental rise of hunting and language argues for language as being a selection of hunting. "Psst. Hey Bob. You go around the hill there and take up a stand, and I'll beat the brush toward you. Maybe he'll come out ahead of me. No...not by the road. Stand next to that tall cedar, behind that old blow down. Yeah. I'll meetcha there."

Against this, the energy benefits of language to a gatherer are minimal.

The growth of social complexity also owes a debt to hunting. As food resources grow limited, a given society will tend to grow more complex in compensation. If there's less energy in the ecosystem, I have to cooperate more efficiently with others in order to procure that energy. And if I go on a gathering expedition with nine other people, I'll still be gathering for my own bag, with my own stick. Hunting alone, I may kill a rabbit, or perhaps an antelope, but only after a number of failed attempts and a great deal of wasted energy. Hunting with nine others, however, I can suddenly herd mammoths into a bog, can set up a drive and ambush, can scout out more country. The energy reward to be found in cooperative hunting is much, much greater than what's to be found in cooperative gathering.

Furthermore, in order to create more efficient tools, better ways of utilizing the available energy, a hunting society would probably devise a rudimentary system of labor division. If Joe's job is exclusively making tools (and they'd be better tools, since he could devote all of his time to them) then Bill, Bob, and Jake can hunt full time without having to bother with tools. The tools would be more sophisticated and the hunters would be more skilled, resulting in more efficient utilizations of energy. Extend this far enough and you're into capitalism.

Relating to all of these adaptations, the expansion of brain size would also seem to be an obvious result of hunting. Tool making, language ability, and social complexity all owe a debt to our need to hunt more efficiently, and all are dependent upon a larger brain. Yet there are a surprising number of academics who find it difficult to accept that we are intelligent—that we are *human*—because of our ability to cause death.

Beyond a certain level, the vegetable resources are as available as they're going to get. Past that level, the only possible expansion is toward other species, other reservoirs of energy. If you are already an efficient gatherer, and if environmental conditions change dramatically, you either begin to eat meat or you go extinct.

We evolved in the semi-arid African savanna after the trees moved away from us. We became predators in this environment in order to more efficiently utilize the limited energy of a limited environment. It seems obvious: We survived because of our ability to hunt.

If our history in predation can be secured according to evolution, it can be established even more firmly according to biology.

Without meat, our bodies lack eight of twenty necessary amino acids. Without meat, we must go to various cereals and legumes, working hard to balance deficiencies of lysine and methionine. Without meat, we must eat unnaturally large quantities of legumes to compensate for the iron loss and anemia associated with vegetarianism. Meat also contains the only source for long-chain fatty acids—necessary for early brain development.

We are dependent upon meat. And if we related to the world in a posture of original intention, we would not be able to survive without it. Chemical fertilizers and genetically modified crops allow for excessive, short-lived yields; refrigerated trucks give the food a quick displacement; artificial preservatives allow peaches and broccoli to be eaten in the same meal with a fall-killed elk. In short, domestication of plants and animals has allowed us to impose our own false systems on the natural world.

The vegetarian does have good intentions. He or she is making an honest attempt to relate more directly to the natural world. The irony, of course, is that in denying our history, he has placed himself *farther* away from the process. *I can reject nature,* he is saying, *I am not an animal.*

It is essential to the process to realize that the engine behind human evolution has been selective death: my own and others.

So what am I, finally?

I am an animal, because I eat and shit and breed and die.

I am a meat eater, if only because there is no animal that has the ability to eat meat that chooses not to.

I am a predator, if only because deer and elk jerk their heads up and run as I walk toward them.

But I'm sitting in front of a computer. It's not unusual for me to read until two in the morning under an electric lamp. This winter my stove and electric heat will place me far enough away from the blizzard outside that it will become merely pretty. Next week I'll drive to Jordan and back in an afternoon whereas it would take me four or five days on foot.

Natural selection outran itself with *Homo sapiens sapiens*. The evolution of language and technology have allowed us to over-succeed as predators, to utilize the energy of our resources with an efficiency that is hardly to be imagined.

It's raining again. Across the way, an eroded bank above the reservoir is slowly collapsing. When I remember it and look out the window, a few more inches are gone. The water below this bank, in a half circle, is noticeably muddier than the rest of the pond.

The Breaks are famous for their dinosaurs. Around the turn of the century, and not far from here, Barnum Brown discovered the world's first Tyrannosaurus. At one time, the Cretaceous sea made an Everglades-like swamp out of most of this country, creating ideal conditions for fossilization. Hunting in the roughest country, you'll sometimes see a bone (much larger than a buffalo's) outlined in an eroding bank. The ground peels away to reveal ancient stories between the layers.

This is a country of incredible age, showing the years in a rare way. But the locals take it in stride. A few have dinosaur bones lying around the house. If you grow up with something it's normal.

I find myself as bothered by the reaction against *Man the Hunter* as by any possible truths in the reaction. Why does anyone *need* to argue that foraging is more acceptable than hunting? Why should killing another animal be bad? *Nothing* beautiful would exist if animals hadn't been killing each other for billions of years. Nothing. We wouldn't exist ourselves.

The fact that the reaction exists at all is evidence of our alienation. It is, I think, part of a larger attempt to impose values on an order that can hold no values.

Projects

At eight in the morning, the Breaks have already been awake for a couple of hours. I step out of the door wearing a sweatshirt (to frustrate the mosquitoes) and comfortable hiking boots. My project for this morning is hiking and scouting, and so the niceness of the day is the principal concern.

A pair of mourning doves whirr down the coulee, preceding me from the base of the barn where they had been feeding on spilled grain. A group of red-winged blackbirds chatter from phone line to tree to phone line, coming to rest finally on the partially submerged limbs of a pine tree in the reservoir. I walk across the yard. The weeds to my right rustle as several somethings run up and crest over a slight rise: three...four immature pheasants, long legged and quick. Two of them, males, are already showing the first hint of color.

A Quiet Place of Violence

There is the same sense of accelerated life around water in the Breaks as in the arid regions of Africa and Australia. An ecosystem is limited by its least available resource; and here, as in other deserts, it's water.

I'm only carrying my binoculars. It's strange, even after not hunting for over eight months, to walk through this country without a gun or bow. It's like pressing in the clutch with your bare foot or signing your name with the wrong hand—the act is familiar but the action is not.

Before the cabin has disappeared behind the first hill, I jump half a dozen antelope: two does, three fawns, and an immature buck. They alternately sprint and stare, startle and run, the patches of white on their rumps flaring in warning. For reasons I can't imagine, the antelope here approach life differently than their flatland counterparts, taking to the trees for cover instead of empty fields, peering back at you from between the branches as if they were whitetail deer.

I walk past them, kicking up a series of meadowlarks and doves. To my right, a short line of round bales interrupts the roll and dip of the field. Beyond these bales, dug into the side of a hill, is one of the original homestead soddies. The timbers have mostly collapsed, the excavated walls have fallen in, but the shape remains. It's only been eighty years or so since it was built. The oldest ranchers might have spent time playing in the yard.

In a sense, any active ranch represents a new order of nature. It must be constantly worked to keep it from falling back into its original state. Windfalls need to be pulled off fences and roads need to be graded. In the winter, watering holes need to be chopped open. Without humans to tend it, domestic wheat would survive only about three years. Domestic cattle, at least in this country, wouldn't make it through a hard snowstorm.

I follow the curve of the coulee down past another, smaller reservoir. This one will only hold water for another few weeks. For a reservoir to be worth anything in this country, it needs a solid bed of clay—any amount of sand lets the water pass on through like a sieve.

A small, two-point mule deer buck jumps up from the downhill side of the dam and bounces into the trees, stopping after a few yards to stare back. Another buck follows behind, stopping almost immediately to see what has spooked his buddy. He's larger than the first, with three points on a side.

The forked horn drops his head to feed. I walk forward and he jerks his head back up. They move further down the coulee, in no hurry.

A ranch road runs over the dam and up the other side, through the trees. I ignore it in favor of following the coulee.

Aldo Leopold defined wilderness as an area capable of absorbing a two-week backpack trip. By this standard, there's very little here that is true wilderness. Some of the deepest pockets might be left untouched for years, but you'll always be able to drive out onto the ridge just above them. But if wilderness is defined as that which is unchanged despite occasional intrusions, then it is here, and in very few other places. Three years ago, we wired a gate shut on a southern border; already, that road has eroded almost entirely away. Small pine trees are growing up between the tracks. Any change in this country is temporary. The Breaks will have it all back.

You get used to a different idea of beauty in this place. It's been one of the wettest summers of the past twenty or thirty years, but the grasses, rather than bursting with chlorophyll, are still pale green, nearly turquoise. The buffalo grass, blue grama, blue stem, needlegrass, sagebrush, and purple smears of flowering thistle are hardy breeds, expecting less water rather than more.

The defining standard is aridity, as in most regions west of the 98th meridian. But the obvious characteristic of water here is not so much its absence as its patient, unreasonable force. By April, runoff has scraped away new runnels of soil, new ravines, new cliffs from a previously mild descent. It's difficult to imagine, during the driest years, that twelve annual inches of precipitation has had the patience to create all this.

Another hundred yards and the coulee blends into another, more sharply defined drainage. These little canyons tend to run between sandstone bluffs. In this particular drainage, the sandstone has been exposed long enough for the wind to have carved it into a row of pillars, small at their bases but expanding into thicker crowns.

I turn up the new drainage. It will take me to the edge of the grazing lease. From there I'll follow the curve of the land back around to the cabin—about five or six miles. Plenty for a morning. The mosquitoes are ferocious.

I'd like to see an elk, but at this time of the year most of the cows and calves are sticking to the heavier cover, and the bulls are in the grain fields up on top, growing their antlers.

A dry wind has picked up from the west.

A couple of miles away, to the south, three white specks move toward the timber—the last of the antelope I saw earlier. I keep walking without bothering to inspect them through the binoculars.

Hiking, as a project, is shallow. And I've been thinking lately about the importance of projects.

We orient our lives according to projects. We largely *are* what we *do*. I see the world through a certain lens if I'm a Baptist preacher rather than a research chemist, a professional athlete rather than a dentist. These are very real ways of ordering the world—and each reality is slightly different from the next.

There's a strength found in life projects that is capable of reducing other aspects of life to trivia. For a project of cattle raising, nineteenth-century settlers will celebrate the disappearance of the buffalo. For a project of westward expansion, the military will intentionally trade smallpox-infested blankets to the Blackfeet. For an insane project of racial purity, Nazis will slaughter six million Jews.

We also orient ourselves to the world according to smaller projects. An evening snow is only intimidating, an icy road is only treacherous, if the morning's project includes a drive to visit family. A mountain only becomes dangerous if we mean to climb it. Frozen ground only becomes hard when we mean to dig postholes. In this way, we make sense of the world.

If you're hiking, nature is something only to walk through and observe. The requirements of the project do not require interaction with the natural world in any meaningful way. You're walking *through* it, not *in* it. For the hiker, the world is...scenery.

If your project is to climb the Tetons, they become daunting, powerful, mobile. They take on a larger dimension. But the birds twittering in the brush as you climb, a rattle of stones around the hill, the slight wind that blows your scent up into a wooded draw, these are distractions to disregard as you move to complete your project. As you hike, nature becomes an object, something to observe rather than participate in. It's required to the extent that hiking through Yellowstone is better than hiking through Manhattan, but this requirement is mostly one of aesthetics.

Furthermore, and more dangerously, we place our personal identity on these projects.

You have a conversation at 30,000 feet, flying to Salt Lake. The guy in the seat next to you asks you what you do.

"Oh, I'm a construction worker."

You identify yourself so strongly with the project of construction that you are able to say, exclusively, that you *are* a construction worker. The climber, as he rappels down a steep face, *is* a climber. If he does it well, he instinctively knows the tensile strengths of certain rocks, the stability of shale slides, the way his equipment can support him—but none of these relate to becoming a part of nature. He is *using* nature to further his projects. The breeze, the birds, the rattle of stones…so much is left out.

The same can be said of nature watching. Worse, since one *watches* objects, nature becomes objectified. The animals you're watching are not fluid members of the natural process—they are passive images.

"Honey, look. A deer! Isn't it pretty?"

Prettiness is mere. Prettiness objectifies the animal, removing it from the essential, pounding, bleeding life that is his and yours, and which is essential to the process.

And if hiking is in bad faith, what about other human activities. Water skiing? Gold mining? Wildlife photography? Taking a picture, the animal and the features of the landscape become pure objects. Within the frame of the lens, they are no longer moving, no longer active, no longer alive; instead, they've been caught as arrested reflections. Nature photography drags from the world a meaning that requires you to stand with your hands behind your back, watching an instant of nature and taking it for reality.

In the early fall, you can drive through parts of Yellowstone Park and watch flocks of wildlife photographers lug tripods and three-foot lenses after grazing bull elk. To most hunters, the kind of process disruption apparent in these domesticated elk is sickening. To the photographer, the animal is merely an opportunity. In fact, it's in the photographer's best interest to promote this kind of disruption in order to have better shots of the elk.

Jacques Cousteau, removed from the world by a camera lens, once said that if he were a hunter he would commit suicide.

So as a project, where does hunting belong?

If a role as predator is *natural* for humans, then the importance of hunting should be found in its relationship to the process. If hunting is your project, you have stopped observing nature and have begun participating in it. Rather than attempting to impose a new order on the process, you have accepted the existing order. Hunting is the project that precludes other projects. It is the original project.

Even farming is more of an attempt to *mold* nature than to accept it. All projects that do not conform to the natural order conflict with it.

The enjoyment of hunting is mostly dependent upon the loss of yourself. The boss giving you a hard time? Your kid using drugs? Mortgage payments? These are superficial projects and will ultimately disintegrate. Held up to the light they are nothing, the guts of a balloon. Only one project fits into the natural order in such a way that Time strengthens it rather than eats it away. Only one project embraces death as essential.

The deer you hunt is never merely pretty. It is *alive*, it is frightened, content, dulled by the rut, *and* it is beautiful. It is beautiful since the order of which it is a part is beautiful.

Hunting is our only project that manages to deobjectify nature, to allow you to participate in it as a member. You walk quietly because you must. You test the wind because you must. You look for tracks in the snow because you must. You notice the way the land lays and how it could relate to you and the potential prey. You search for broken branches and scrapes. You watch the deer come up the draw toward you, noticing how easily it moves, how it fades into the hillside, how it is a living, feeling, bleeding part of the natural order: like you. And then you pull the trigger because you must.

"What do you do?"
"I'm a hunter."

I've turned away from the Breaks to start walking back toward the cabin. Without having realized it, I've picked up speed. My project is cabin return, and so I'm no longer even looking out past the borders of the road. I'm hungry, and it's almost lunchtime.

I laid some chicken filets out to thaw last night before going to bed, so I'll be having a grilled chicken sandwich. Physical needs always take precedence over abstractions. It's hard to keep your attention focused on good ideas if you're hungry, sexually aroused, or have to go to the bathroom.

Of course, we've spent more time within the process *being* hunted rather than hunting. And this seems to fit. The ultimate hunts are those in which the relationship between you and the animal is mutual: you hunt him, he hunts you. Polar bears have been known to circle around and stalk tracking hunters; during the early days of African colonialism, lions followed the construction of the railroads, feeding off the workers; somewhere, there's a photograph of a leopard staring down from a tree, a paw resting on some poor soul's disarticulated limbs.

But this is the way it should be. Eating and being eaten. We're not the culmination of creatures—we are only one exotic flavor. We *will* become something else; it just takes the right catastrophe. We're nothing special.

If I deny my animality—my roles as predator and prey within the process—then I have denied nature itself. And the process cannot be denied. Not without destroying it.

But there's a problem here. If humans are animals, how could we produce anything that is outside the process? If nature produced us, aren't we, as animals, subject to the order regardless of what we do? If the problem is extended to its logical conclusions, we would have to say that humans are either completely natural, including New York City, acid rain, and George Will, or we are completely unnatural, in which case we shouldn't have to eat or shit or breed or die.

But if nature is a process, then we can have it both ways. Yes, we are animals and yes we are connected to the world, but we are capable of producing things that lie outside the spheres of reciprocation. Henry Ford the individual was natural, Ford the car was unnatural. George Will is natural, his column is not.

We could, like the poet Gary Snyder, force a distinction between nature and wildness, in which case New York is natural but unwild. But this is ultimately a different way of saying the same thing. Humans implicitly are wild, but capable of producing tamed things.

Fortunately, we do have one available project that refuses to alienate us from nature, that conforms to the process. Hunting is the only "natural" thing I have left.

Things

Time's passing quickly, in a way peculiar to country bachelors, cloistered priests, and academics on sabbatical, spreading rather than passing. Unclocked. It's mid-August, which means that hunting season is coming like a train, and I've been practicing.

I'm going out with a recurve this year for the first time. In previous seasons, I've used a compound, but I've lately found an appreciation for the silence and simplicity of a non-mechanical bow: the smooth tension of the pull, the sound of air running through feathers like a falcon diving, the thump of the arrow on the target.

I draw, and the arm that grips the body of the bow is slightly bent. I anchor the string at my cheek and release as the innate measures of accuracy click into place. Unlike a compound, the recurve allows you to hold the bow at full draw for only a breath; you have to manage a shot *in the split second after the elk has seen the movement of your arms.*

I've been practicing for thirty minutes a day. My fingers, behind the smallest joint, are developing blisters. Practice is necessary: Hunting and mercy are not exclusive states.

An elderly friend in the east, a retired minister, spends his time giving lectures and demonstrations on instinctive bowshooting. This man will shoot masking tape out of the middle of tossed-up washers, will hit dimes, will pulverize aspirins in the air. The idea is to familiarize yourself with the bow to such an extent that conscious thought only intrudes.

But consciousness intrudes everywhere.

Today I'll screw the target points off my arrows and replace them with rubber blunts. I'll walk, and as I walk, I'll shoot at non-specific targets—drawing and firing and trying to cultivate an awareness that so far I haven't been able to find.

I drive a couple of miles into Spring Creek, a section on the south edge of the ranch, and park beside an old school house and stock pump. There are enough cottonwoods to make the road shady and cool.

I leave the truck behind and walk through the trees with my bow. There's the black end of a small stump, ten yards away. Whack. The arrow bounces back crookedly, fletching end slung up. I walk to retrieve it.

What exactly is estrangement? Is it to be found in clothes and basic tools? Or perhaps fifty-dollar haircuts and eyeglasses? Somehow, I don't think so.

The West has canonized the pursuit of comfort, but this isn't where we find estrangement, either.

I think it means simply not being able to fully

comprehend the larger truths of nature. Haircuts, eyeglasses, and Porsches are just manifestations of our incomprehension. The largest truths are, for the most part, unremarkable.

I put an arrow into a knothole; it sticks there, quivering. I shoot at an upright piece of shale on the ground, but since I'm proud of that last shot, I miss. The arrow bounces into the brush, turning over.

In Europe, bow-and-arrow technology is about 15,000 years old. In North America the technology was discovered about 2,500 years ago.

It would seem that technologies like this are a principal element of estrangement, either product or cause. Can we fully realize ourselves as part of the process if we're screened behind technology?

Product or cause. The mind creates the technology. Could a mind within the process ever think up the internal combustion engine? On the other hand, could any mind survive in its original condition if it had to face the Brooklyn/Queens Expressway each morning?

Technology has almost always interceded between the animal and hunter. The hunter has always manipulated the environment with tools. The *idea* of technology can't be the problem.

Sioux boys, if they got caught stealing meat off their mothers' drying racks, would punish each other with hits off a prickly pear. Warriors would use the juice of the cactus as an astringent, helping to close wounds. Girls would make toy tepees out of cottonwood leaves. Porcupine quills were used for decoration. There was nothing in their society that wasn't profoundly connected to its source, nothing that wouldn't return immediately to its original context after they were done with it. In the Arctic north, some tribes had over one-hundred uses for walrus ivory, using it for everything from dog-harness buckles to tent-line tensioners.

After 1600, the Gros Ventre and Assiniboine shared the Breaks as a hunting ground. Three hundred years ago, every shot I made with this bow would have been a direct result of my knowledge of the process and my role within it. The wood would have been selected and cured by my own hand and knowledge. The string would have been sinew from a buffalo that I had killed. The arrows would have come from a cottonwood and the arrowheads from traded obsidian. Technology was the result of my knowledge of nature and my role within it. It neither produced nor caused estrangement.

A yellow bloom of sweet clover, backed by a rotting log. Whack. Again, whack. Again, whack. Missing each time. I'm in my head too much. I retrieve the arrows and begin walking uphill, out of the ravine.

In one of the seminal philosophical treatises on hunting, Ortega y Gasset has said that hunting is a "contest or confrontation between two systems of instincts." He points out that the only things that escape the animal's "sensibilities" are those things that are unnatural. As it should be understood, unnatural means beyond the process.

The massive eruptions of human technology are not only beyond the process, they *force* us beyond it through their use. I relate more strongly to the animal I hunt, instinct to instinct, if I'm on foot rather than in a truck, carrying a bow rather than a rifle, a recurve rather than a compound. Extremes of technology force a levee between two competing instincts.

If the purpose of hunting is only to kill an animal, then the process is moot; we contain the technological ability to kill all animals. The *project* may be to kill an animal, but the project is useful only to the extent that it allows us to orient ourselves to the process. This is true to some degree for even the most corrupt hunters.

One hundred yards out of the trees, moisture has diminished, replacing sweet clover and cottonwoods with prickly pear and sage. I take aim at a single cactus in the middle of a patch and shoot wide.

Ortega also points out, in the same work, that hunting is dependent upon scarcity of game. Scarcity is *assumed* in the very act of hunting. If game were superabundant, he says, then there would not exist that animal behavior which we distinguish as hunting. The example he uses relates to the most common activity of all: Since air is abundant, there is no technical ability involved in breathing. We don't hunt air.

Although Ortega doesn't touch on it himself, the logical extension of this idea of game scarcity is the necessity of limiting technology.

One of the larger image problems hunting has recently experienced relates to the misconceptions of those who haven't hunted, who see only the semi-domesticated whitetails grazing in their backyard and the .308 with a seven-power scope. The logical conclusion is that hunting is a bloodthirsty, simple activity. We step out the back door, shoot something with a cannon, and step back in.

Unfortunately, technology *has* allowed killing to become an act of effortless shooting. If you hunt from a lawn chair, the deer has become nothing more than a target that jumps around a lot. Extremes of technology force new definitions and new distinctions on the act of killing an animal. There must be a difference between simple, objectified killing and true hunting.

Your neighbor who drives up the road the first day of season to "get his deer" isn't hunting. He shoots a doe from the window, snaps a picture, and takes it to the butcher for processing. The deer is easily acquired and disposed of as an object, in part because of the distancing found in technology run amuck. It's only by consciously limiting our technology that we can engage in the same act for which we have been biologically cultivated. It's only by creating a self-imposed scarcity of game that we can fully relate to the process in our role of original intention.

So walking is better than driving, a bow is better than a rifle, a recurve is better than a compound.

Of course, if the game is especially scarce or if it's very capable at eluding the hunter, then higher levels of technology become proportionately justifiable.

Game scarcity also relates, perhaps less strongly, to trophy hunting. What kind of hunt is involved in shooting a spike or a doe? There is a drastic overabundance of these animals as related to our ability to kill them. So again, we must consciously limit ourselves. We are hunting, but there should be one very scarce type of animal to attract our skills. And the trophies with the largest racks, the oldest, the wisest, are almost always the most difficult to kill, even with the best of equipment.

The need for this kind of limiting, however, is

moderated by the need to actualize a kill. The project must be *valid*. In the same way that a mountain climber has to be climbing with the *intention* of reaching a certain point, the hunter has to be hunting with the valid *intention* of killing an animal. If the climber can see that the peak is inaccessible anyway, then why work to orient himself with the mountain, why climb that last stretch of cliff if he has to turn right back around?

The project must be valid in relationship to the difficulty found in actualizing it. If you're lazy, start walking. If you're a very good rifle shot, move to the bow. If you can shoot in the kill zone five times out of six from sixty yards, think about picking up a spear and atlatl.

A diminishment of technology lessens the distance between you and the animal, distilling the hunt down into a measure of instincts. A gun may exist at the shallow level of technology, but as a hunter holding the gun, you are operating on a more profound level. The hunt is not something that happens to the animal by chance, as Ortega points out. Instinctively, the deer has anticipated my stalk. Just as, instinctively, I've been stalking my entire life.

Our technology has developed beyond the ability of the environment to reciprocate, allowing what would otherwise be inconceivable killing. Between 1872 and 1874, more than three million bison were killed on the Great Plains. Ten years later, only 300 hides were shipped east. This is a startling and horrible reflection on hunting, until you realize that the man who could kill two thousand buffalo a year wasn't a hunter at all…just a shooter of objectified animals.

It's been called giving the animal a sporting chance. What it really means, however, is relating to the animal in an original role of intention. The small four point taken after a season of hard hunting gains a value disproportionate to its size. Killing a 380 point Boone and Crockett bull elk is ethically abhorrent if it was shot over the hood of a truck while it was crossing out of Yellowstone Park. We are predators, and our project of predation is natural. But we are also rational. And rationality implies control.

If trophy hunting is permissible, perhaps required, what about trophy display? Putting trophy heads on a wall has been one of the most visible and easily-reviled aspects of hunting. Is it justifiable?

One thing is certain: If the animals are used as a way to further other projects, then mounted heads are not ethical. There is no way you can use them to say, "Look at what *I* did." The animal has then become a pure object. But as good as hunting can be, and as nicely as it can return you to the process, there comes a time when you have to return to technology-tainted society, to air-conditioned buildings and honking cars. If you can look up at the animal, perhaps take it down and heft its horns, then you and that small piece of yourself you left back in the woods are, for the moment, together again.

Photographs don't cut it. They're two dimensional, static.

The sheep I killed hangs to my right, above the computer. I remember the smooth, oily texture of the foam form and the heft of the horns as I screwed them in place, the smell of glue and the way the wires behind the glass eyes pierced the foam. But when I look up and *see* the sheep, what I remember is the rainy, flaccid chill of my skin and how blood trickled from its neck—the same blood that was on my hand. I remember the way it stuck its head up over the rise to look at me, curious in the way only sheep can be curious. I remember the way we studied each other in the moments before I shot it.

And now, as I write, I'm almost crying.

The only tribute I can pay it now is to watch it for the rest of my life: remembering.

Trophies should be kept under lock and key, with the door opened only for a rare-because-precious story. The hunter should softly tell his story about *that* elk, the one up there, using his hands and face to draw from the empty air some image of his hunt. He is telling you about life—not in summary but in *essence.*

One of the blisters on my finger has popped, dripping down and turning the palm of my hand wet and bloody. I walk back to the truck, taking automatic note of my own tracks and the scratch marks where one of the arrows skipped.

Driving back across the ranch, mosquitoes mob the windshield and outside mirror, beating themselves against the glass.

In the end, technology fails in three ways: It is unreciprocable and beyond the process; it creates a false sense of game abundance; and it clouds the connections between instincts.

Still, I'm holding my bow. The broadheads I shoot will be steel razors. The binoculars around my neck are blatant intrusions.

I live in an alienated world and have to devote the largest part of my time to making a living. Technology allows me to make up a difference that would otherwise be accounted for by more time spent in the field. Is there any way to reconcile this? Is there an obligation to work *toward* an ideal of perfection, even if that ideal is perfectly unattainable?

Marinetti said in 1909, "Light, noise, speed, you can never get enough of these." Within the intervening decades we have come full circle, until this generation might begin the same epitaph with, "Twilight, tranquility, hesitation, give us more of these." Rather than a diesel bus blaring through an intersection, a pool of water with rising fish has become our ideal.

The beautiful, good things of nature survive in the Breaks because we haven't had the opportunity to contaminate them with our cancers: the bulldozers, shopping malls, airports. What we have in the Breaks is a remnant of a changed world.

The ranchers have passively accepted the harsh conditions of the Breaks even while strongly supporting technology. Their lives are hard, and there's a noticeable potential for gadgets to make them easier.

Down in Lost Creek, an old International truck has been left to rust. Elsewhere, it's not unusual to see graveyards of old farm equipment half hidden behind screens of ponderosa. Several wooden boats have been left abandoned on the shores of the lake. Warnings. This is what might happen. The Breaks are patient, but we have numbers.

I park the truck and walk to the cabin, leaving my binoculars and bow on the seat. I close the cabin door against a darkness that will begin before the sun has entirely set.

Language

There is a tendency to romance that which is lost or inaccessible: childhood, old loves, great wealth.

At this moment, I simultaneously exist in the past, present, and future. I am the man who is writing this essay, I am the child who killed a mountain lion, and I am the unmarried husband who can love his unborn children. We have our timeline of repressions, fears, and hopes, and these are what we are. But the past exists by itself and is, for this reason, an idyll.

Strangely, the written word exists in this same, flat dimension. Hamlet is forever holding Yorick's skull, Leda is even now loosening her thighs to the swan. Like the past, the word is dangerous and not to be trusted. Iago is evil, incomprehensibly evil, evil with a certainty to which the living can never aspire, and he will never be otherwise. If the bedtime word insists that Heidi is innocent, that Gollum is corrupt, then it must be: it *is*.

What I have in mind now is the incredible power of language. Of naming.

The ability to name ourselves has distinguished us, at the moment of naming, from the rest of the world. *Humanity* demands that there be an *inhumanity*. I name myself, and I have presupposed the existence of an Other. When I name myself human, that means that there must be an inhuman. When I call something natural, there must be something that's unnatural. Naming appropriates, naming controls, naming diminishes. A sunset, when described as red, becomes *only* a red sunset.

Naming is powerful. "You're a *bastard*," an old girlfriend hisses in the parking lot, and you feel a number of emotions: sheepishness (that you *are* a bit of a bastard), anger (that she should call *you* a bastard) and rebellion (you're *more* than that).

Naming is one of the principal features of a dichotomy that dominates every aspect of our lives: that of subject and object. When I say, "I," I declare myself a subject. I am the person that is perceiving the world. And the world that I perceive is made up of objects. There are trucks, trees, and fields. There are computers, calculators, and pencils. Each of these objects is largely dependent upon me for their existence, or at least for a perception of their existence. It is impossible for any of us to imagine a world without ourselves in the middle of it.

We are all aware of the idea of a right triangle. Yet this idea does not exist away from us. Close your eyes and imagine a right triangle. Where is the 90-degree angle? Lower left? Lower right? It's always *someplace*. We're always standing in front of it, watching it, creating it, objectifying it. It cannot exist away from us, away from our subjectivity.

Psychologist Jacques Lacan devoted most of his work to language study, and a concern with subjectivity takes on the largest measure of importance in this work. For Lacan, there can be no subject before symbolization. In other words, before the child starts talking, she isn't aware of herself as a separate entity. How could she possibly conceive of herself as an "I" when she can't even say it?

When I first say my name, or your name, when I point to my own existence apart from yours, I am placing myself away from the world. When I say *truck*, when I say *deer*, I am establishing myself as a subject in front of an object.

Objectification creates the potential for violence. War propaganda is nothing if not an attempt to justify violence by objectifying the enemy. In Vietnam we fought "gooks" and "chinks." We *didn't* fight Tham Nguyen, who had a little boy and two girls, who had spent a year at Seoul University and hoped someday to go to medical school. That would have been admitting that he was a person, that he contained his own subjectivity. It's much harder to drop bombs on a person.

The destruction being done to the environment has arisen from our objectification of it. If we're not a part of it, why not destroy it? Elk and deer, elephants and gazelles, no other facet of the process has a conception of itself as existing apart from the world. If they can't say it, they can't think it. We are the only thing in the entire process that has the ability to imagine an "I" apart. It is possible to envy animals their probable consciousness of inclusion—where the social and human "I" has been lost to the mythic "we." Where human language has been fragmented in the face of an infinite, mute moment.

But if language separates us from nature, how can we possibly move beyond it?
One of the arguments against hunting has been that it's part of a larger objectification of the natural world. It's been argued that it is only possible to shoot an animal after it has been objectified. Hunting, however, is not an objectification of the natural world, but the purest form of *deobjectification*—one in which the entire dichotomy of subject and objects is lost within the act.
Hunting is our only possible relationship to another species that is *prelinguistic*.
All other relationships reconstitute the language-based subject/object dualisms. We talk to our pet dog like it's a child, expecting it to do what we tell it. We throw hay out into the field and call the horses like teenage boys. We *name* our pets in an attempt to place a conscious identity on them: *You're* Blackie, okay?
But hunting is beyond dualisms. Instead of dealing with the prey linguistically, the hunter is made aware of the elk on a deeper, more archaic level: that of predator to prey. The odor of elk was a taste in your mouth, and you could taste nothing else. You walked, and your feet made no noise through the damp leaves. A bugle came at you through the fog. You stepped forward into it, and there was suddenly nothing else in the world.

You stalk, and as you stalk you are aware of the elk's strengths and its weakness, particularly as they relate to its abilities to elude you. You move and you stay still. Move and stay still. How can you stay still so long? The project demands it. Like almost all species, the elk notices movement. Blink twice and it's all over. You slow your breathing until you have cultivated, without knowing it, something close to a meditative consciousness. You empty yourself, offering your name to the act. You slip between the bones of a juniper and its bark.

And the elk, as prey, is constantly aware of your capacities as a hunter, unless your technology exceeds its evolved expectations. The elk has no need to leave its skin because it has no idea of owning a skin. It has no language and no idea of existing apart. This is what you're up against—not a single animal but a chain of them, a circle of strong hearts bound together. The cow elk watching you from the end of the herd is watching for all elk.

Nothing to do but close your eyes and slice, holding the mouths of your wrists out for acceptance. Is this enough?

The entire relationship exists on a level beyond language. By hunting, your life moves away from subjects and objects. You're part of a relationship larger than either of the two animals involved. You're no longer precisely yourself. Hunting requires you to lose yourself in the act.

Not that this is any great revelation. Most acts of skill require a loss of self. If you stop and think how you're going to hit the tennis ball, you've already lost the point. But what *is* a revelation is the absorption of the act by the process. You lose yourself in the act and then the act is lost in the natural order. How wonderful!

If the hunt is experienced on a level beyond language,

A Quiet Place of Violence

how could you possibly communicate it? And if you can't communicate it, how could you justify it? Or institutionalize it? Language is the stumbling block to an understanding of hunting. We literally do not have the words to describe what is happening.

Ludwig Wittgenstein, an early twentieth-century language philosopher, argued that language is a social phenomenon. A group of students each has a small matchbox. One by one they open their private matchboxes, and say, "I have a beetle in my box." But how can we be sure that the boxes all contain beetles? My idea of beetleness may be entirely different from yours. The only way we can confirm the existence of the others' beetles is to share the contents and say, "Yes, that is what I meant by 'beetle' as well."

Since your relationship to the process is entirely personal—in nature, there is no equivalent Other with whom to compare beetles—it must be extra-linguistic.

Our only possible experiential relationship with the wilderness, our only possible way of avoiding the subjects and objects of language, is through the hunt. Photography, hiking, mountain biking, biology…they all reduce the environment to a level of objectification. They are projects of alienation.

It's a symptom, I think, of the estrangement found in language that poets have become the voice of a new appreciation of nature. If language separates us, we need new words. Poets like Gary Snyder and Robinson Jeffers have helped shape our modern view toward nature in the same way that their romantic predecessors shaped our previous views.

Paul Valéry, a French symbolist, wrote, "To see is to forget the name of the thing one sees."

There are no words to communicate the experienced meaning of hunting and killing an animal.

Religion

Sunday morning and I'm facing west. The rising sun warms my back. As I watch, the pines across the ravine change color abruptly from their pre-light grays to fresh, pulsing greens. It's difficult to think of color as anything other than the object to which it is attached, but this green is as much a part of the rising sun as it is the tree. Without light, there would be no green, just as without the tree there would be no green. Perhaps without an eye to see it there would be no green, either.

Is there some common substance, some wellspring or aether, out of which both light and tree arise? Or perhaps some more ultimate source, containing within it light and tree and eye? Even though we've named the world and its laws, we are a part of them as well. We are part of the world, that is, until we realize that we are watching, that we are naming, that we simply *are*: awareness and our *ability to say "me" throws us out of the loop.*

The truly spiritual act is that which seeks to lower this dike of self-consciousness, even if only for a moment. The Buddhist conception of no-mind and the meditational practices designed to achieve it both point toward this levee. The Biblical command in Thessalonians, "Pray without ceasing," is a doctrine of the same order. Both point directly to the Taoist virtue of "not doing."

I stand and walk further down the ridge. My shadow stretches down the hill to my left, warped by the nip and tuck of the bank. This ridge isn't part of Lost Creek, not officially, but if I walk far enough down, it will become Lost Creek. Already the lake is visible, and beyond that, the Little Rockies. Further to the west, I can just make out the Judiths. Both ranges seem much closer than they are. It's one of the virtues of a dry climate: clarity of vision.

I stop on a small point, the last high spot before this small ridge spreads down into the larger basin. Across the way, in a small saddle between eroded banks, a bit of white catches my eye. Through the binoculars, I make out the bare skeleton of a mule deer fawn, lines of red still tracing the recesses of its vertebrae. You can read the story: Coyotes surprised it as it fed through the saddle, or chased it into the saddle, and were able to catch it as it tried to run up the steep banks. Life!

Rationality has forced us away from a historical creator. Adam and Eve are clichés. At the same time, knowledge has been able to bring us closer to mystical awe at the simple purity and power of the world *as it is*. On top of the mountain, looking down, we say, "My God!" Although God isn't precisely what we mean. "It tugs at my soul," the purple poets say, although soul isn't just what has been moved. It's just that we contain no other vocabulary to express what we feel.

The value of spirituality isn't found in questioning the existence of God but in the postures of humility and concern that give rise to the question. These are the virtues that every religion worth its oats commits itself to. And while the question itself is natural and necessary and wonderful, the *answering* of the question is dangerous and diminishing. Like the red sunset, a description of God—*any* attempt to formalize God's intentions—lessens the value of the question. Any movement away from the individual, any movement toward the institution, is corruption of a good thing.

It's still difficult for some to realize that we weren't created in a burst of light and an opening of hands, that our relationship to the natural world is more than trap doors and hidden mirrors. We are part of the world, not its rulers.

Technology and language have been behind our estrangement, but in the West, all the news is that Christianity has done the same thing.

Christianity assumes separation by giving humans domination of all that flies or crawls. Within the traditional Judeo-Christian cosmology, this domination means that the world exists *only* for us. Even now, evolution, ecology, and Einstein haven't been enough to completely remove us from the pinnacle of God's attention. A contemporary cowboy poet writes that when God made Montana, He said, "I will make lots of grass / For cattle and sheep; / The minerals and oil, / I will bury them deep."

And after it assures us that the world was made only

for us, to save or damn as we please, Christianity follows Plato in its belief that what we're living in now is only an ugly reflection of a greater One, a perfect Beauty behind everything. Unfortunately, if nature within and without is a reflection of something more divine, then it has already been corrupted. If the next life is all that matters, then the good things in this life are to be ignored.

But the Christian alienation from nature reaches deeper than this. Frederick Turner, in his influential work *Beyond Geography*, points out that the earliest Israelites were *delivered* from the wilderness into the promised land. Nature was a power to run from. A thousand years later, Paul drew a strict line of separation between the natural world and the religious, between the body and the soul. In Romans 6, he exhorts us not to "let sin exercise dominion in your mortal bodies." And in Romans 7:18, he writes, "For I know that nothing good dwells within me, that is, in my flesh." He goes on *ad infinitum*.

Jesus's messages were beautiful in their simple calls to love. But after Jesus, the shapers of the church seemed determined to show nature as contemptible.

Like language, it's almost impossible to transplant a religion. Doctrines are tied inextricably to place. Spiritually, the God of manna, locusts, plagues, and rivers of blood has little business in the Breaks.

Many of our current environmental problems have been traced back to the Neolithic revolution—to farming. As demonstrated so well by Paul Shepard, agriculture trades small-group egalitarianism for ruling chiefdoms. It leads to more contagious diseases, earlier menarche, about three times as many childbirths per woman, and poorer general nourishment. But landholders, bureaucrats, and

A Quiet Place of Violence

politicians all benefit from a settled, agrarian existence, and these are the people who call the political and religious shots.

Christianity developed as an agricultural religion. And it is the religion that conquered the New World.

From his second settlement in Hispaniola, Columbus forced the native Arawaks to bring him, every three months, a small copper bell filled with gold. Those with no access to gold (and there was very little gold on the island) had their hands chopped off. Within two years, between the executions and mass suicides, 125,000 to 500,000 Arawaks died.

In his first report to the King and Queen of Spain, Columbus wrote, "Thus the eternal God, Our Lord, gives victory to those who follow His way over apparent impossibilities."

Before Columbus, there were between four and twelve million Indians north of the Rio Grande, speaking 550 languages from nine distinct linguistic groups.

An agricultural religion of domination and exploitation simply couldn't adjust to the passive, egalitarian needs of a culture still so close to its hunting and gathering origins.

We tend to resist the notion that the hunter-gatherers could have lived better lives than ours. But this resistance comes primarily from a misconceived notion of social Darwinism. It must always be remembered that societies change, constantly change, but that natural selection is based upon physical development rather than cultural. Since a culture will always promote *itself* and its characteristics as the epitome of social evolution, there is no possibility of consensus. If I argue that advanced technology is evidence of our superiority, a Yanomami might just as easily argue that it is evidence of our *inferiority*, since it has allowed us to lose touch with the earth.

But if God lets me hold the Truth, then cultural relativism goes out the window, and I can commit any act of atrocity in order to make *you* see the Truth.

Christianity began to lose its stranglehold only as rationalism forced us away from the unconditional acceptance of its doctrines. In parting with creationism to favor evolution, we were finally able to realize the spiritual value of nature itself.

In 1836 Ralph Waldo Emerson anonymously wrote his essay *Nature*, preceding the publication of Darwin's *On the Origin of Species* by thirteen years. Here was a man well versed in the use of words like "spirit" and "soul," yet still capable of writing, "Know then, that the world exists for you." He wrote that "the universe is composed of Nature and the Soul," but that nature is all that is "NOT ME." Even in 1836, after realizing nature to be beautiful and valuable, Emerson's God was monastic, anthropocentric, and controlling. His "pure idea" in the mind, his spiritual aesthetic, resisted all disagreeable appearances, "swine, spiders, snakes, pests...."

Aesthetically and spiritually, Emerson's nature was a pure object.

His protégé, Henry David Thoreau, published *Walden* eight years later, moving a few steps ahead. For his time, Thoreau's insights were profound. Where Emerson found God *through* nature, Thoreau looked for God *within* nature. But still, he refused to see himself as a *part* of nature.

He wrote, "We are conscious of an animal in us, which awakens in proportion as our higher nature slumbers. It is reptile and sensual, and perhaps cannot be wholly expelled...we may be well, yet not pure." His instincts for fishing he calls a "lower order of creation," and found, when he ate fish, "something essentially unclean about this diet...." He objected to "animal food" because of its "uncleanness," and considered that person blessed who was "assured that the animal is dying out in him day by day, and the divine being established."

Thoreau's idea of spirit was set apart from his own animality. If God was in nature, he was only there to watch on our daily walks. Furthermore, only some parts of God were to be accepted, the rest being too dirty or too low to be suited for such a high being as man. Thoreau went on to reject hunting as an action that should be left behind as one acquires certain sophistications.

So long as nature is seen as something apart, then it will exist only for us. If we are observing nature, then it gains value only through our observation. God is still giving nature to us on a silver platter—it's only the face of God that has changed. If nature needs a subject to make it complete, it has been objectified.

In the tradition of Emerson and Thoreau, John Muir, a naturalist and non-hunter, was undoubtedly one of the most spiritual *observers* of the natural world. He would spend weeks in the Sierra Madres and Yosemite, would camp in forests of Sequoia, would wax eloquent about the greatness of God and the elegant balance of nature, but then would eat only the bread and fruit that he had brought with him. He was largely responsible for the creation of Yosemite National Park and the Sierra Club, but he would go hungry rather than kill another animal. He loved nature and found it valuable, but he would only watch it from a distance, worshiping it, refusing to participate in it.

Observation of any sort, even observation through the soul, reconstitutes the subject/object dichotomy. For

Muir, nature assuaged what Emerson called a "nobler want of man," supplying, as at least one scholar has put it, "an *object* for soul, will, and intellect."

If nature is beautiful, serving a spiritual purpose through its beauty, then it is most certainly *not me*.

This is what we've moved beyond and through.

The sun has risen enough to warm the ground, waking up the mosquitoes. I lather my face and hands with repellent and lean back against a pine tree. If I were hunting, if I were sitting here with a bow or rifle, I would be forced by my project to stay awake and attend to every small movement in the coulee, every rustle of grass. I would certainly not be sitting in the sun. As it is, I lean my head back and think more about the spirit.

Hunting refuses to exist entirely on a spiritual plane. If it did, spiritual non-hunters like Muir would be a problem. If you are a spiritual hunter, you have come to it only after experiencing the actual hunt.

If spirituality is seen as following a doctrine, then hunting doesn't qualify. There are no creeds to restrict freedom and promise Hell for those who disobey, no preachers to lead the less enlightened of us by the ear. But if spirituality means love and a felt connection with the world and the desire to give of yourself, then hunting is not only our most natural activity, it is also our most spiritual.

Whether sitting on dojo cushions, kneeling in prayer before a cross, or standing on the edge of a field with a bow, it's the same "spirit" that is being stroked. Love, connections, selflessness—they all exist between the life to be taken and the final point of the arrow. And these moments are themselves suspended within a series of actions that, together, have been condemned as barbaric and cruel.

It's true that even the most adamant antihunter can approach nature spiritually. Yet an ache of the soul doesn't legitimize a point of view. Spirit is universal. Inclusion is rare.

If I'm hunting, I am no longer *using* nature; I *am* nature. I am no longer worshiping God; I am part of a larger, coalition of gods. The best hunters, although grinning at the mention of Buddha or Lao Tzu, come closer to incorporating the ideals of these men than do most eastern scholars.

Use leads to objectification, even if it is use for spiritual gain. Non-hunters and anti-hunters can enjoy wilderness superficially as Thoreau's *sanctum sanctorum*, an idealized escape from that which they find impossible in their own urban lives. Emerson, Thoreau, John Denver... idolaters chanting mantras toward an ideal. And their very idealization is an objectification. That boy from the country who talked to birds and animals? It turns out he *was* insane.

But hunting, now...it's the greatest kind of pantheism, to hunt and accept the order that exists prior to your own. We are not *using* the woods to cultivate our souls, we *are* the woods.

I wake up with a stiff neck and a braille tragedy written on my face in bark. My eyes, where I had put less repellent, are a raccoon ring of swollen, itching mosquito bites. That'll teach me.

It's fitting, given this discussion, that Thoreau has

written some of the most quoted lines in the animal rights movement: "Every creature is better alive than dead, men and moose and pine trees, and he who understands it aright will rather preserve its life than destroy it."

No one who had fully realized the value of hunting, who had felt himself to be part of the natural order, could have made this statement.

More rightly, the lines should read: "Life is built on death, men and moose and pine trees, and he who understands it aright will not reject death by unnaturally preserving life."

I sit awhile longer. I just sit. Ignoring the notebook on my knees. This is the hunter's luxury—free time. Only farmers have to work from daylight to dark, cultivating their bread.

The day progresses, the sun moves west and starts to bleed.

Native Americans had something over us in their ability to spiritualize the animals they killed. Their animals had personalities, existing on such a higher plane that they had to be pacified and cajoled.

A people's myths are their umbilical tie to the land. In the east, the Algonquins saw the animals as the embodied power of the earth. The world was created when a Great Hare, floating on a wooden raft, took a grain of sand (brought to him by Muskrat) and formed the earth. The Blackfeet, Arapaho, Gros Ventre, and Cree all believed in Napi, the Old Man. When the world was water, Napi was brought a ball of mud by a muskrat; he blew on the mud until it swelled and grew into the earth. To live on the earth, he made birds and animals and humankind and taught the humans how to hunt and gather.

Our spiritual myth hangs bloody and tortured in a million churches around the world. He was a noble, generous spirit, but he had nothing to do with the Breaks. And unlike Raven and Deer, he was more concerned with the afterlife than this life.

Instead of *living* myths, where Raven creates, Wolf saves, and Deer teaches, we have a very dead one. And he belongs in Jerusalem, not the Missouri Breaks. What's a little ozone depletion? What's a little spotlighting? Jesus didn't say anything about spotlighting. In fact, he didn't mention deer or coyotes at all.

Even today, if a Pueblo Indian kills an animal, he first purifies himself and then hums or sings as he hunts, asking the deer to be willing to die for him. After killing it, he cuts off the head and turns it east, sprinkling corn meal before its mouth and praying to it for forgiveness.

The trick is neither to abhor nature nor to worship it, but rather to be a spirit among spirits. The Oglala Sioux received their sacred pipe and seven rites when a strange woman appeared among them, handed the stuff over, and turned into a red and brown buffalo calf that, in turn, grew into a white and black buffalo. There was no clear line of distinction between the human and the animal. Seventeenth century missionaries reported that one of the hardest things to make the natives understand was why they should have souls but that animals should not.

With our split inheritances of western rationality and Christianity, we can't *really* believe in a Native American plenum of spirits. But perhaps in place of these myths we could mythologize ourselves.

To put it another way, natives humanized nature. In order to be more deeply connected to the land, they made

Raven talk and Buffalo dance. And since they were a *part* of the world, and owed their existence to it, they had to give it their respect. If our background of deified rationality won't let us raise the world to the level of God, how about raising *ourselves* to the level of the world? How about hunting our way through the wilderness?

Sunday *evening and the very, very faithful are on their way back to church. They'll miss a fine red sunset.*

Preparing

*I*t's a familiar emotion, this mix of expectation and excitement, triggered each year not so much by the hunt as by its associations.

The opening of bow season isn't for another two days, but tonight I'll get things ready, and tomorrow I'll boat across the lake into a new area. Until the first herds are pushed down from the grain fields, the ranch won't be much good for elk. Since I'll be camping, the preparations will happily be taking longer than usual.

First, the essentials. I set out my down sleeping bag before anything else—heavy for this time of the year but I can always stick a leg out. To go under the sleeping bag, a thin roll of foam. Beside the bag and foam, my old three-man tent.

In the kitchen, beside my bags of food, I set out a number of small items that comfort has made essential.

Toilet paper's the big one, and after that a change of clothes in case it rains. Since it's been so unseasonably wet, I include a light raincoat, and because I always get tired of beans and granola after the first day, I pull out a fly rod for Fort Peck bass. In the same bag with the food, I drop a small pump bottle of mosquito repellent and a smaller bottle of hydroperiodide pills for giardia. I'm taking along a five-gallon jug of tap water to keep in camp, but you never know.

As an afterthought, I also throw in a stray bottle of lighter fluid. It can mean the difference between going to bed wet and cold or warm and dry.

For the hunting itself, I lay out my bow and six arrows, the feather fletchings recently waterproofed. Beside the bow, I place my old fanny pack. The fanny pack will hold a water bottle, a roll of cotton rope, three plastic garbage bags for meat storage or emergency raincoats, my skinning knife, a whetstone, a Bic lighter, a collapsible saw, and a simple first aid kit.

My camouflage outfit is in the closet, but there's no point in getting that out until tomorrow morning. When it's warm like this, I'll typically wear a long sleeve, light-cotton camouflage shirt over an undershirt, and a pair of light cotton pants. For the past few years I've also worn a brown felt hat, used variously as a pillow, an antelope decoy, a bow target, a pistol target, a fire fanner, a trail marker and, on one memorable occasion, a fire-on-the-pants-leg-putter-outer.

To carry all this stuff I have a frame backpack with a removable outer shell. I wear the empty frame as I hunt, the filled fanny pack tied across the bottom. This setup allows me to carry all that I need in the field, but also gives me extra room when it comes time to pack out meat and heads.

I wear the binoculars around my neck (usually tucked into a shirt or jacket pocket to keep them from swinging) and a .357 in my fanny pack. Marlin Perkins meets Bill Hickok. The pistol carries five slugs with the hammer resting on an empty chamber. There's no real need for the pistol—the bears are gone and you can always walk around rattlesnakes—but if an animal I have shot with the bow is slow in dying, I feel an obligation to end it as quickly as possible. I'm not sure of the legalities of this, but to me the higher-law necessity is final.

Finally I carry a grunt tube on a shoestring around my neck. It's little more than a length of flexible plastic tubing with a fabric cover for camouflage, but when I bugle through it with a three-reed mouthpiece, it gives the call an essential depth and resonance. The call itself is a horseshoe-shaped piece of plastic with three layers of thin rubber stretched across the inside, designed to fit between the tongue and pallet. It can be used for turkey gobbling, coyote calling, cow elk mews, and, of course, bugling.

All of this stuff. As a kid, I thought that to go camping you just needed feet. I entertained complicated visions of running away into the hills behind our house to live off boiled-bark tea and dandelion steak; I would turn up months later with a rippled jaw and bloody moccasins. Twenty years later, it turns out that you need a loaded travois just to take a turn around the block.

Still, it's not as much as it sounds. Importantly, most of it relates to the periods before and after the stalk, and so very little of it disrupts the accord between hunter and animal.

I change my mind and take out the camouflage shirt

and pants from the closet, hanging them from the knob on the front door. Then I move them to the top of the door at eye level.

Tomorrow the hunt begins, although not the hunting itself.

For no reason other than the ritual, I will get up at five o'clock. The owl that's been hanging around the house looking for rabbits will still be making its abrupt screeches; the Big Dipper, decently low in the sky when I went to bed, will have swung around to the other side. I will shiver as I walk from the kitchen to the truck, carrying my bow and pack. The pack will go in the bed of the truck, the bow in the back of the cab, and my binoculars on the seat beside me. Rather than slamming the truck door shut, I will push it softly until the metal clicks into place.

This is a larger tradition.

I will go back inside and fill my battered thermos with coffee. The windows will be dark mirrors. The cabin, after I turn out the lights and leave, will go back to its own business.

I'll wish it were colder so I could scrape the window, just for the sound of ice against metal, the warmth that comes from watching snow melt against your glove.

Could there be anything more holy?

Purposes

Driving down into Devil's Creek, I blew a tire, which put me behind by an hour. The wind had picked up by the time I had set the boat in the water. And it was drizzling rain as I erected the tent on the other side of the lake, the kind of steady shower that would make it impossible to get back to the cabin if I broke a leg or burst an appendix. But that's all part of it. It's hard to believe that this is the same desert as last year.

With any luck, the weather will clear by tomorrow. Not that there would be any real harm in having to stay a few extra days.

Behind my tent to the north are the twin buttes I'll be exploring. The Breaks run up to them in radiating lines. From this angle, the timber seems sparser than on the south side. To the east there's a series of bare, sheepy looking hillsides that might be good to check out from up *on top of the smaller, western butte. But I'm not making any real hunting plans. I'll just get up there and see.*

I unzip the tent and hurry over to the stack of wet driftwood I gathered a few hours ago. For supper, I'll stick a can of beans in the fire (which would have been impossible to start without my lighter fluid) and eat a can of peaches. Blue and red flames hug the wood as trace chemicals from evaporated water melt and burn.

The idea of project is the defining element. But I'm not up to getting into that one, not right now.

It's lonely sitting on the shore, with the rain dripping through the seams of my rain coat. The larger drops hit the rim of my hat like small pistol shots.

Hunting is a social activity. There's no denying that. Loneliness forces it home. Most of our modern rituals seem to center around low, eager voices in the morning and stories at night. But if the importance of hunting is to be found in the relationship between the individual and his prey, why is hunting so socially complex?

And without meaning to, I'm back on the idea of projects.

There's a split, here. The project may be to kill an animal, but the larger purpose should be to orient yourself with the process.

You're a mountain climber, again. Your *project* is to get to the top of the mountain, but this isn't your *purpose*. If it were your purpose, you could charter a helicopter to fly you and your flag to the summit. Your project may be to get to the top, but your larger purpose is the creation of an accord between you and the mountain, or the ego-satisfaction to be found in conquering a peak. Whatever. Anyway, what's important is that you can only fulfill your purpose by having a project that orients you with the mountain.

In order to kill an animal, to fulfill our project, hunting with others can often be more beneficial than hunting alone. But the *purpose* of the hunt, at least within the last few thousand years, has been to orient ourselves to the natural order. Killing an animal at all costs is no more reasonable than flying a helicopter to the peak. The social aspects of the hunt might therefore sometimes work against the individual benefits. On the other hand, the only way we can begin to orient ourselves is through a valid project. The mountain must be steep enough to force you into an accord with it, but not so steep that the peak is unattainable.

We need to exist among the world's projects, accepting them rather than appropriating them. While a ponderosa pine exists in-itself, with its own ends and reasons, a telephone pole exists only because we need it to hold up wires.

We are measured by our ability to complete projects. "He's a good worker," they say. "Does everything he can to put food on the table." Or, "He's the best quarterback we've had for years." Athletics, politics, business, academics—all of these measure our ability to complete our projects. The importance of goals is endlessly stressed, but how often does one stop to consider *why*. It turns out that "goal" is almost an exact synonym for "project." Goals are a way of orienting ourselves with the world.

We are hunting because of the project. And the project has been given to us not by society but by the process.

Hunting is not a sport. Competition treats the animal as a means to an end, objectifying it.

But hunting is a *pure* sport. It presents our athletic

abilities in the context in which they first evolved. Bob from next door can step out and shoot his deer, but it takes true excellence to kill a seven point bull elk or a thirty-four-inch mule deer with a bow.

Nicely, the distinction between sport and nonsport fits the distinction between project and process. Sport is project. Nonsport is process.

Why does the pulse quicken at the sight of an exceptional mule deer buck stepping from the juniper thicket? How could evolution possibly account for a predator that hunts only rare animals? If I'm suited by evolution to hunt for food, why can't I get excited at the sight of a fawn walking across my lawn?

It's the way we orient ourselves to the project that changes, not the project itself. "Buck fever" is much the same feeling you get before the big game, or before you finally decide to call and ask her out. Your stomach twists up into your throat because you have worked hard toward the completion of a deeply-felt project, and it's about to be fulfilled. Or not. If you were stalking a fawn with very primitive technology, and if your own life and the life of your family depended upon making the shot, the buck fever would be just the same.

Within the elastic affinity of the stalk, we are entirely alone with the animal. We are breathing together, feeling the other's pulse through the ground. Who could say that this is *merely* a sport? The distinction has to be emphasized. The project, the sport, allows us to orient ourselves within the natural order. But the order that produced the sport requires our first allegiance. And this is the process.

But there's a danger here. If we're hunting only for the project, only to reach the peak, then it becomes possible to reduce the relationship back to one of subjects and objects. If the animal is *only* a trophy to be taken, then we've ignored the process by objectifying the animal.

The animal must never be a means to an end. If you want to acquire a trophy so badly that you're willing to do anything to get it—if you let the project take precedence over the process—then the animal has been reduced to an object, a means to an end. It then becomes possible to use such extremes of technology that true hunting was only something you did when you were a boy with a BB gun. Ted Kerasote, in his book, *Bloodties*, followed a group of professional hunters into Siberia for snow sheep. One of the hunters, a candidate for the Winchester Award, shot a sheep driven to him by a helicopter.

If you are exclusively a trophy hunter, your new project does not return you to the natural order, it places you further beyond it.

The process must take precedence, if only to temper the project.

I'm suddenly tired and hungry and my fire has gone out. And I'm lonely.

Loneliness is much more palpable on the shores of an empty lake than on the couch at home. Fort Peck has a shoreline of almost 1,600 miles, and if it weren't the first day of hunting season tomorrow, I would almost certainly be the only one camping on the lake.

Tomorrow...is the first day of hunting season.

Hunt

The rain hasn't let up like I'd hoped it would. But nobody ever said you had to be comfortable. So I'm not.

I'm sitting under a pine tree on a small ridge. If the sun were out, I would almost be in the shadow of the butte. I've been sitting here long enough that my garbage-bag seat has grown holes.

I rest my elbows on my knees and glass the open hillsides across from me for the third or fourth time. Nothing. I swing around. There's my tent. A brown bubble just beyond the fingers of the water. I look at it again through my binoculars just to look. Do we ever lose our childish fascination with these things?

I'm glad I waterproofed my fletching. Do they ever field test this stuff?

As I shift, pieces of dirt crumble away from the bank and skitter down the slope like mice. On these wet, steep hills, if moisture exceeds the angle of repose, pieces of gumbo can roll and build like large snowballs; you'll see them sitting out in the middle of a ruined field the next day, trailing broken wheat like exhaust.

Nothing's moving. Everything with any sense is watching the rain from under a pine tree. If I were rifle hunting, I'd be kicking through the top edges of these wooded draws, hoping to jump something out. With the bow, your only chance lies in seeing them before they see you. I should get back, but it's hard to give up.

As a predator you adjust yourself to your prey, in almost precisely the same way that the prey probably adjusts itself to their predators. If you're hunting bear, every blackened stump is a rounded shoulder; if you're hunting elk or deer, every forked branch is a pair of ears, every CMR sign a white rump.

I imagine our prey species recognize us, their predators, largely by our faces. Like lions, wolves, and owls, our eyes are set in the front of our heads, allowing for binocularity. We use this binocular vision to sight, track, and pounce on our prey. Deer, rabbits, and gazelles have eyes further around their heads, and so are able to tell when something is sneaking up behind them. In order to distinguish between the real and the imagined, movement becomes the distinguishing criteria. In the Breaks at just this moment, nothing's moving.

There's been some sign. Just back down the hill there was a set of smallish tracks that could have been sheep; on a little promontory a hundred yards further around there was a clump of juniper recently stripped of bark, probably by an elk.

My chances are slim, but I would still like to top out over the butte, just to see what's on the other side. It's only a quarter mile or so away. I dig the palms of my hands back into the hillside and push myself up.

At the top of the ridge, I hear a quick, muffled drumming. It stops as soon as I find firm footing and stand to listen. In less than a minute it comes again: a toy drum on a stick.

Around the fringe of a juniper thicket a few hundred yards up the hill, I catch a flash of white. Through the binoculars, I can just make out a brood of sharptails hunched under the branches, their feathers fluffed and their heads sunk down into their wings. As I watch, one of the younger ones stands on its legs and flaps forward, shaking off the water. The wings flash white; its chest drums.

I pull an arrow from my quiver and replace the broadhead with a rubber blunt. A spitted grouse over the fire would be wonderful.

Hoping they'll stay where they are, I drop down out of sight and begin to approach them from the bottom, around the corner of the juniper. Within forty yards, I can hear them chuckling; within twenty yards they begin to shuffle, restless. I rise up from my knees, already drawing my bow. I briefly take in the arrangement of birds under the branches and, without stopping to consciously aim, I focus on the closest bird and release. A quick hiss of wind, a thump, and then a grouse is flopping in the wet grass, wings askew. The rest of the covey flushes, and sets their wings to coast down the hill toward a stand of pine.

I run up to the grouse and capture it under two hands. Its strength waning, it is still able to twist and scratch cold feet at my hands, to beat one wing against my chest. My arrow didn't penetrate but seems to have broken a wing, perhaps the ribs. In one quick motion, not unlike opening a bottle of soda, I twist the bird's neck. It trembles, and for the first time in its life, lies entirely still.

I take out the tattered bag I'd used as a seat, find a sound length of it in the middle, and wrap it around the bird. I tie it off and thread it through my belt loop. I'll clean it at the tent.

The dead weight swings against my hip as I walk. I wish there was something else to be done, something to show my appreciation. But reason doesn't allow this. Appreciation to whom, to what? The bird's dead.

The ridge line feeds directly into the butte through a random series of sandstone pillars; on a horizontal surface, they would look like a setting of chess pieces. The bare ground between them has been scalloped by an intricate series of trails. As I turn my way up through them, something unseen clatters away above me.

You always have to concentrate. The mind-crap disappears—the phrases of popular songs and interior arguments fade away—only when you force yourself to realize that an animal could always be over the next hill.

Before I expect it, I'm climbing up onto the crest of the butte. It is precisely flat, and although the sandstone is interspersed with timber, the top is bare. I turn around. The lake stretches out left to right, dominating the view. Through the binoculars, I can't see my tent but I can just make out a sandstone formation that might be my predator's perch above Lost Creek.

The top of the butte is only a few hundred yards wide. I walk across to the other side. The UL Bend, flat and dry, stretches away to the west. The Breaks crumble away to the east. In front of me, only a few miles away, sit a pickup and camper. From Glendive, probably.

That's all. I'm wet and cold and there's nothing else. I'm going back to camp.

I'm thinking of the next step. If the value of hunting lies in its relationship to the process, then it is this relationship that must provide the basis for more subtle considerations.

I've lately been handing out truths like cards, smug and self-assured. But I'm not sure I'm happy with much of what I've said. I believe it, but I'm not happy with it.

So much blood is on my hands—I could paint walls. And it was a revelation to discover the blood *on* my hands is holier than the blood *in* my hands.

Hunting is a deobjectification of the animal. The act of killing is the final stage of deobjectification. The grouse swinging at my waist *is* the world. Tonight I'll go to bed feeling that I have been a part of something complete.

In the West we tend to celebrate our projects only if they have succeeded. And perhaps this is also why project must never take precedence over process. It's unavoidable for any hunt to contain equal measures of success and failure. Your deer got away. Failure. But what if he didn't get away? Is this what it was all about, this blood and dying and cold flesh? Again, failure. Your deer got away. Success! Thank it for being the more capable. But your deer didn't get away. Again, success! You have conscionable steaks to eat this winter.

We should finally learn to hunt beyond even the terms success and failure. We need the project in order to orient ourselves with the natural order, but the project's fulfillment is only necessary to the extent that it must be valid. Its ultimate success is not required—only the possibility of its success.

I have a base from which to expand, but a base does not answer the fundamental question of ethics: "Is this right?"

Historically we have hunted. We have developed as hunters. We have had to hunt in order to survive. But now we no longer *have* to hunt. We can survive without it. We can go to the grocery store and pick up our processed, bloodless hams and chickens. If I have no choice, my action is neither moral nor immoral. Breathing air or drinking water are not moral concerns. With the ability to accept or reject the hunt, the idea of hunting ethics has gained a terminal relevance.

Of course, the animal you're really hunting is the animal within yourself, buried under the layers of light, noise, and speed. If left undisturbed under this shell, you will finally come to believe in nothing past it—no fresh air, no growing leaves; and worse, you'll believe that such things never existed. But if caught in time you can take a breath and consider how strangling the air inside had been, how tepid. And if you begin hunting…then! Then you dwindle, fading with each step into the ropes of grass around your legs, into the smell of pine and wood smoke and the taste of rain. You hunt until you have forgotten even your own name, losing it in the plenum of names, the diaspora, the fabric of unspoken words.

Part II

Quiet Violence

Ethics

I have been across the lake and back. In three days I saw a cow and a calf, a spike, two deer, and four bighorn rams. The rams were beautiful. I sat and watched them from a mile away and, because I don't have a sheep tag, they were merely beautiful. I ran after the spike but found nothing beyond his tracks.

For these nine animals, I walked close to thirty miles. I walked blisters across my heels and pulled a muscle in my back. And then driving back to the cabin last night—insult to injury—I found eight deer camped out in the lawn; they flushed away from my headlights, bouncing down the coulee with great bounces.

The nights are much cooler than they were just a week ago. The mosquitoes are in some nether world of their own, waiting for the next warm spell.

One thing more: I just heard my first bugle of the season.

I took a walk around the outside edge of the ranch, finally spotting a five point feeding on the edge of an old burn. A single, unexcited bugle rose from the trees behind him. If the five point is the satellite bull, then the herd bull, the bugling bull, will be larger.

Walking back, I startled a mule deer buck up out of the trees and onto the evening skyline. He was just under thirty inches wide with deep, curving forks and a pair of non-typical points that pushed away from the main beams like broken fingers.

And now I can't sleep.

Tomorrow will be the first real hunt I've had this year; the first legitimate project. I will walk away from the cabin in the dark, carrying my recurve and four arrows, one of which may kill an animal. I might bugle. If there's a reply, I'll move toward it with the intention of killing. And it will be right.

It will be right.

Philosophy as a discipline is concerned with the basic questions—what is beautiful, what can we know, what is real. Ethics—what is right—is perhaps the most relevant to our daily lives. Before we can act rightly, we must be able to recognize what right action is.

At its foundations, the study of ethics must have begun as a means of justifying those acts that were already known to be right. I know, but I don't know.

Murder may be wrong, but why?

Well, because society would fall apart if murder were acceptable.

Stealing may be wrong, but why?

Well, a free market society wouldn't function if everybody stole from each other.

After the obvious questions are covered, the base can then be extended to more ambiguous actions. If cold-blooded murder is wrong, how about killing in defense of your home? How about accidental killing? How about hospital euthanasia? In this way, the maxim created as lip service to an already-answered question can be used to cover more subtle problems.

An ethic of hunting might arise in the same manner. I know that inclusion within the process is good, and I know that the only path to inclusion is found within my role as a predator. So what now?

Over the past two centuries, nature has suffered unimaginably, and largely because we haven't had an ethic to treat the environment as anything other than a means to an end. So long as you don't step on your neighbor's toes, you've been able to kill whatever you like, plow in any direction, extract any fossil fuel or mineral that made a profit. And this has failed. It's failed to the tune of the possible extinction of over one hundred species a day. It's failed until the quality of most human lives has degenerated into exhaust fumes and cold cement. It's failed until we can see how our own species might become extinct in the not-too-distant future.

In the same way that social ethics is designed to protect society, a process ethic must be designed to protect the natural world. And if hunting is part of our larger, human relationship to the process, this ethic must be a subdivision of a larger, all encompassing ethic.

What is right hunting?

Hunting codes exist universally, family to family, club to club. But even at their most hopeful, codes only skirt around real ethics. As early as 1873 the first American journal directed toward the hunter and conservationist, *Forest and Stream*, made a distinction between the "true sportsman" and the hunter who shot birds on the ground or water, who killed only for meat, who poached, or who shot for the market. This man was reviled for being unsportsmanlike, but no other reason was given.

Codes typically reflect a sensed, unverbalized ethic. We know, but we don't *know*. Challenge is important, but why? Because it makes it harder. But why does it need to be harder? Well, so we can get in shape and prolong the enjoyment of the hunt. You shouldn't kill unnecessary numbers, but why? Well, to keep the populations healthy. But why? Well, so our grandchildren can enjoy hunting.

The answers seem reasonable, but they're incomplete. Any code that refers only to the hunter himself contains no teeth at all. If I'm acting a certain way only for my benefit, then there's nothing to keep me from acting in some other way. So long as the hunter is the only concern, then there is no possibility for a real ethic. Moral agents must come at least in pairs.

*T*here's a late half moon tonight. Reflection, even half reflection, is enough to see by. These thoughts are going around, and I'm in no mood to stare at the ceiling and wish that I could sleep.

I grab my jacket and hat and step off the porch. A nighthawk calls across the lake: a deep, belching call designed to carry long distances—more like a toad than a bird.

In many ways, darkness contains the hardest essentials of the Breaks, exposing the waxy threads of instinct. In this darkness, even the deer can't be seen—they're just there and then they're not. Deer bounce heavily, elk run full out, cows rustle, and it's cheating to bring a flashlight.

Until recently ethics have always been social. According to tradition, if I were sealed away in a bubble or dropped off on a desert island, it would be impossible for me to act either ethically or unethically.

And ethics require action. An ethic that promotes inaction is no ethic at all. Ethics require that we exist and act in terms of the Other. The reason for our action is no longer self-contained.

Ethics include rights and obligations. I may have a right to ranch this ground undisturbed, but with that right, I have an obligation to extend the same courtesy to the rancher next to me. How a system of ethics approaches this idea of rights and obligations is what distinguishes it from its predecessors and inheritors.

It's only as our culture has realized the damage being done to the world that we've come to realize the need for an *environmental* ethic. But if ethics have traditionally been tough, how much more difficult must an ethic of the environment be? The questions then not only encompass the problem of killing (always a sticky issue), but other species as well, sentient and non-sentient. We don't really know what death is, much less an elk. Or a grasshopper. Or a ponderosa pine.

Until this most recent expansion, ethics were entirely social. And in their first attempts to create a new ethics, environmental philosophers made the logical step and wondered if social, moral agency shouldn't be accorded to all animals. Why should I have more of a right to live than a deer? They feel pain, and they're innocent, too.

It was the easiest jump, but also happened to be the most potentially dangerous.

The road curves around the rim of a small ravine and carries me forward. A great horned owl takes wing to sail in absolute silence across the road. I walk on, stumbling across the occasional stone. At the end of the road I touch the mailbox—an instinct left over from high school wind sprints.

Aristotle began it all with a book named after his son: *Nicomachean Ethics*. In this work, Aristotle is concerned with fostering the habits of men: the first call to right action. He believes that the aim of life is to find happiness, and that this can only occur by fulfilling our potential. Since he defines man as the "reasoning" animal, he says that we can only find happiness through our reasoning ability. Who are the happiest people? Philosophers, of course. He also gives a doctrine of moderation in which he says that since each situation requires action potentially too great or too small, right action must fall between the extremes.

Aristotle is curious largely for his influence. Things heat up only after the Renaissance.

Jeremy Bentham and John Stuart Mill are the most prominent founders of that eighteenth and nineteenth century branch of ethics called utilitarianism. Utilitarianism judges actions based on the measure of produced happiness and pain. The aim of ethics, they say, should be to gain the greatest amount of happiness and the least amount of pain for the greatest number of people. This is often stated, somewhat erroneously, as, "The greatest good for the greatest number." An action is right insofar as it produces the greatest possible social utility, and wrong insofar as it reduces it.

As opposed to utilitarianism, which finds morality only in the *results* of an act, Immanuel Kant's categorical imperative is concerned with the *intentions* of an act. Although Kant puts it several different ways, his ethic essentially says that one should "act only on that maxim which you can at the same time will to become universal law." In other words, an ethical act is one wherein if everyone acted in the same way, society would flourish, and an unethical act is one wherein society would disintegrate.

In 1971, John Rawls, under Kant's strong influence, published his important work, *A Theory of Justice*. In this book, Rawls proposes a "veil of ignorance," and places behind this veil a number of hypothetical adults, ignorant of all aspects of their life. Their sex, race, financial status, favorite color, all disappear and they are left only with their rationality. Would these purely rational people choose a society in which members of one race were discriminated against? Several of them might turn out to be racial minorities, so they wouldn't advocate this system. Would they choose a society in which one of them held 80 percent of the wealth and the rest were impoverished? Obviously not.

Rawls comes to the conclusion that behind this veil, the people would say that each of them has a right to pursue their own life plans without interference, and by connection, the obligation of non-interference into the life plans of others. There is an inherent moral worth within each individual that must be respected. From this foundation, a just society can be created, based ultimately on Kant's doctrine of universal law.

There is a fundamental difference between these philosophies. Utilitarianism is a *teleological* philosophy, judging an act by its end rather than by the process leading up to that end. Kant and Rawls propose *deontological* systems, finding morality in the intentions behind the act, regardless of the outcome. Utilitarianism would see no moral distinction between intending to kill someone and intending only to scare them, if both actions had the same result. Deontology would say that intending to scare someone is more permissible than intending to kill them.

It needs to be stated clearly: A deontological ethic is one of intentions.

For most of my life I've hunted with either my father or brother, and I've come to believe in the existence of something vital between the two people who hunt often together. You grow attuned to the other's actions, the other's sounds. You find yourself acting as a tensile receiver, gaining information by the sudden freezing of his muscles, the jerk of his head.

But hunting alone is, in many ways, more essential. You rely only on yourself. The eyes that will see the game are your eyes, and the faults to be made will be your faults. There's nothing, not even another hunter, between you and the animal.

Hunting is both a social and an individual activity, and so an ethics of hunting must blend the ethics of nature and society, unhinging its jaw to include all situations.

The first mistake would be to focus attention on individual animals. The process cares nothing for individuals. If we're going to protect the system, we can't look toward components of the system but toward the system itself. Typically, the animal rights activists in their ignorance of

A Quiet Place of Violence

nature, do not look beyond the individual. If an animal is feeling pain, that's all that matters.

Ecology and evolution define the boundaries of the natural order, dictating the necessity of preying and being preyed upon. To disrupt these two relationships is to erode the essential web of nature itself. When death is seen as evil, or if pain is something to be rejected at all costs, then nature itself is threatened. If most animal rights activists had their utopias, neither ecology nor evolution would exist. An ideology would reshape and potentially destroy the idealized nature it is designed to protect.

Deontology and teleology are the blocks that we have to work with. And they each have their shortcomings.

Almost without exception, the animal rights activists have chosen utilitarianism as their basic doctrine. It's a philosophy easily expanded to include other species of animals. Why not, after all, give an animal's pleasures and pains a weight equal to our own? If pain is bad for me, why shouldn't it be bad for a deer? And if I can be happy, why can't a deer be happy?

There are several, traditional problems with utilitarianism, apart from its uses as an animal rights philosophy. First, it allows the sacrifice of individuals. If America gains an overall utility by executing homosexuals to slow the spread of AIDS, then, according to utilitarianism, such executions would be moral. It's also an ethic that's difficult to put into practice; how do you measure abstractions like happiness and pain, particularly in animals? And are we so sure that happiness is the "good" to be measured. Deer evolved in a prey role. If you remove them from that role, what's left?

But the standard pitfalls of utilitarianism are insignificant when compared to the potential disaster found in giving individuals of nature a greater value than nature itself.

Morality is meant to be a force of stabilization, not disruption. In this regard, it's necessary for a social ethic to say that death and pain caused by someone else are ethically unjust. Society must promote harmony. But within nature, caused death and pain are essential. Without them, nature itself wouldn't exist. The death of grass allows a deer to live. The death of a deer allows coyotes to live. Together, the death of trees, deer, and coyotes allows the grass to grow. Within the process, death is the standard that must be ethically protected rather than fought against.

Out of context, this pronouncement sounds ridiculous, even dangerous. An ethical protection of death? But it's dangerous only when looked at through a lens ground by traditional, social ethics. Human pain caused by other humans is repulsive because society has had to insure certain patterns of behavior from its members. Christianity, the Bill of Rights, and Kant's categorical imperative have all retroactively fulfilled a need for a stable society. But now we find that in order for the environment to survive, we must fulfill another need. The law has been laid down for us: death is necessary, death is good. Now we must formalize the law.

Unfortunately, we've come to see all forms of death and pain through the rose-colored spectacles of society.

Ortega y Gasset has noted the difference between social violence and predation. Socially, in what might be called loud violence, the intention of an act is reciprocated. The lion fights the lion, the human fights the human, and violence is intended on both ends. If loud violence proliferated, our species would fail, so social ethics has evolved to insure that it doesn't. But the relationship between a predator and its prey exists on a different, quieter plane. Ortega writes, "Fighting is mutual aggression. In hunting, however, the question is always that of one animal striving to hunt, while the other strives not to be hunted. Hunting is not reciprocal."

Humans are not inherently violent creatures. We are predators, but predation exists within the natural order while violence exists beyond it. Loud violence estranges us, and quiet violence is the state from which we've been estranged.

Until now, the stability of the natural order has been assured without our interference. And so we have had the space to grow preoccupied with loud violence, creating elaborate systems of ethics to channel our attention. But in the flurry we've ignored quiet violence. Utilitarianism ignores it in its teleology and Rawls and Kant ignore it in their life plans.

We must create of nature a moral entity dependent neither on the teleological worth of an act's results nor on the deontological worth of the individual. But then the ethic must be either deontological or teleological.

It's a problem.

Happily, the debate is decided by nature itself.

The fluid, evolutionary characteristics of the animal, the periodic extinction and creation of species, the necessary trophic movement of energy from mouth to mouth, all point to a worth of the system over the individual. Although I will die because of the nature of the process,

I could not have lived had it not existed. The whole is much larger than the sum of its parts.

And there can be no teleological goal behind the process. No state exists that can't be transformed into another. There is no end to be caught and assayed and termed moral or immoral. It's true that everything in nature dies, but it's equally true that nothing is ever finished.

Although deontology finds inherent worth in individuals and actions, and although individuals within the system can hold no inherent worth, the system itself might be called moral. The way animals relate to each other, the process of their relationship, contains qualities that hold an individual worth. The process is moral as a whole.

Nature is, and can only be, deontological.

I sit on the porch and take off my boots, dropping them on the packed dirt; the ground absorbs the noise. Emily Brontë wondered famously, "how any one could ever imagine unquiet slumbers for the sleepers in that quiet earth."

Philosophers have excelled at creating elaborate explanations for what is often taken for granted. The basic split between deontology and teleology is really nothing more than the difference between processes and plans. Hunters see themselves as part of a larger, fluid system: deontologists. The animal rights activists see themselves as fighting unjust acts in the interests of a larger plan: teleologists. The previous codes of hunting have focused on the intentions of the hunter (trophy hunting over meat hunting, sport over market, etc.), which are deontological. The beliefs of the activists have centered on the final act of killing—the blood and pain and ending of life—which is teleological.

Since hunting means participating within a system that holds an inherent moral worth, the ethic of hunting must be deontological. Not that this is a problem; Modern hunting has always been deontological. Intentions have always been taken into account. All of us are aware on some level that the hunter's acts, if divorced from intention, are meaningless: the animal is dead, regardless. It is the approach to the animal which is necessarily moral or immoral.

Evolution and ecology nicely support this idea. If killing an animal in an atmosphere of hunting and gathering is permissible (as evolutionarily it must be), then arguments against non-subsistence hunting must rest on the hunter himself, and how he approaches the animal.

The animal rights activists run into a wall here. They cannot reasonably argue that hunting was okay ten thousand years ago (because the hunting was done in the interests of basic subsistence) but isn't today (because the animals we hunt feel pain). The activists are simultaneously trying to argue a deontological position (a hunting and gathering *approach* to the animal was fine) with a teleological position (the animal's pain, the *result* of the hunt, disallows hunting).

Deontology would allow every animal to continue to exist in its role as either a predator or a prey, eating and being eaten. Every animal is the way it is because of its relationship to other animals—the constant flux of more easily preying upon other creatures or more skillfully avoiding becoming prey.

We have two spheres of ethics, social and processional. And if the purpose of ethics is stabilization, then each of these spheres must function according to different laws. While killing might destabilize society, and is almost always unethical within that sphere, within nature it is actually a force of stabilization, and so must be defended. Hunting, since it is now a choice that we can reject or accept, has become an ethical consideration. And if the process is dependent upon killing, then within the natural sphere, some form of hunting *must* be ethical.

Still an activist howls from the balcony, "But how could hunting and killing an animal ever be moral?"

And the answer, whispered out of respect for this ultimate truth, is, "But how could it not?"

Rings

I begin walking from the cabin at five thirty, shivering in a light camouflage shirt that's too warm after a few minutes. A rain that's almost a fog soaks through my shirt; water sloshes in my boots, heel to toe. I almost turn back, but last night's bugle pushes me on.

Clay collects on the soles of my boots. I kick my feet forward, sending grass-stubbled chunks of it through the air. I top out on the road, breathing hard, and a new wind sends my scent down into the grain fields. Not good. Then it switches and blows into my face. Worse. Occasionally, a breeze swirls around in these draws like a trapped bird, letting everything know that man is in the woods.

I get an idea in my head and I can't let it go.

It's easy to say that the process deserves moral worth, but it's much harder to justify. The process has no inherent structure of rights and obligations that would recommend it as a moral agent. It doesn't even have the ability to act morally, since moral choice is based on free will. Even right and wrong, these basic, fundamental ideas, exist only as human ideas. All evils, all goods, all concepts of evil and good, are brought into the world only through the human animal. How could nature possibly be moral?

The act of hunting creates boundaries. Today, I'll stop my hunt with a kill or darkness. But philosophy destroys boundaries. Most philosophers, the good ones, spend their lives only trying to more fully realize that first and last teaching of Socrates: to know that you don't know anything.

If nothing else, there is an unquestioned ethic of resource management. If my life project includes fishing mountain streams for cutthroat, I have a right to do this without someone else building a pulp mill at the head of Slough Creek. If my project is logging, I have a right to log, but only so long as it doesn't interfere with my neighbor's project of elk hunting. In this scenario, the process and the animals within it are entirely objects to be manipulated to another end. It's an unfortunate reality that most game laws treat animals this way, giving them respect only through their human hunters. As bad as this idea is, it's the place to start.

I walk around a little further, hoping to find a windless area to stand and listen for a bugle. The road drops behind a patch of trees and the breeze eases up, though doesn't disappear. I wait, hands in pockets.

A Quiet Place of Violence

The first real attempt to approach the natural system as anything other than an object came in 1949 when the ecologist Aldo Leopold published his famous "land ethic." We are members of a community, he said, and we must have respect for its other members. It was the first attempt to endow the natural order with a deontological, moral worth. It was a brilliant first step—looking beyond the small individuals, including himself, to realize the importance of the larger system. Written very simply, the land ethic says, "A thing is right when it tends to preserve the integrity, stability and beauty of the biotic community. It is wrong when it tends otherwise."

This was the first, and still the best, systems (or holistic) philosophy. Unfortunately, it has been ignored by most philosophers as presumptuously amateurish, by most other academics as heartless toward the plight of individuals, and by the larger public who have obstinately refused to see the need.

Damn! Over my breathing, down off to the side, brush is breaking. The wind has blown my odor down into the fields. The show's already over.

But as I listen, what I had thought was brush turns out to be antlers cracking together. Two bulls fighting!

It's hard to judge the distance, but they can't be more than a few hundred yards off. I slow my breathing, absorbing the sound.

After a moment the wind shifts and I ease back up the road and off the edge, hoping to circle around and come up on them from below.

Some supporters of Leopold's land ethic have

unfortunately argued that the process comes first and that's that. If the system is the good that needs to be protected, shouldn't we protect it at all costs? Under this logic, since five billion people are more than the process would naturally support, we ought to remove about 90 percent of them.

In response, two promoters of Leopold's Land Ethic, Richard Sylvan and Val Plumwood, have envisioned the natural development of ethics as a series of "annular" rings. An ethic develops to accommodate a certain need, they say, and as the horizon of society changes a new ring develops to speak to the new need. The stone-age family had an ethics that it adhered to, but as a tribe grew up around it, a new ethic grew with it. While it might be okay to punch my brother on the shoulder for no reason, it wouldn't be acceptable to just go up and punch another member of the tribe.

As the tribe was absorbed into other tribes, a new set of duties and obligations arose on top of the previous sets. The idea, as Sylvan and Plumwood (and following them, J. Baird Callicott) have argued, is that our obligations to the old rings don't change (I can still punch my brother on the shoulder), but we do have new obligations to the next ring. In this way, Leopold's land ethic simply represents an expansion of traditional ethics, not an entirely new departure.

Under this analogy, my obligations to civilization don't change, even as the telescoping series of ethics comes to include the process.

I've emphasized humanity's estrangement from nature. Have, in fact, beat it into the ground. We have sealed ourselves away, and this is all. In order to artificially maintain populations vastly larger than any ecosystem would normally accommodate, we process our feces and urine, genetically alter our food to make it more abundant and transportable, exorcise personal parasites like demons, and hermetically seal our bodies away in steel coffins to quietly turn to ashes, removed from even the smallest benefit to the process.

Leopold paved the way by showing us that if the need is felt, and if the existing structures don't accommodate the need, then the structures themselves must be changed. It thus seems only reasonable that the concept of moral agency must be expanded.

Nature cannot choose to act morally. It is beyond ethical questions. But if we can benefit from it, and if it can benefit from us, then it could perhaps be said to exist as a *passive* moral agent, returning both benefits and harms to a set of active agents: to us.

As the active agents, our behavior determines the character of the process's reflection. Simply put, we treat the process well and it treats us well. We treat it poorly and it treats us poorly.

But since it can be called a moral agent, every part of the process must be given consideration—even that which has no direct, human relevance. Mosquitoes and cockroaches must be seen as viable parts of the process even though they do not benefit us and even occasionally hurt us.

Without humans, moral questions wouldn't be questions. Nothing would act ethically because nothing could choose its actions. But if nature passively reflects our actions, then it gains morality without the necessity of choice. A mirror, after all, reflects precisely what stands in front of it.

Nature must be given the right to exist apart from us, even while cutting its moral revolutions within our collective shadow.

*T*he sun won't be rising for another fifteen minutes, but I can see well enough to make out the space through the trees where the bulls must have been fighting. They've moved on.

The rain falls harder, pulling a batch of mosquitoes up from the grass, catching me without repellent.

At the lower end of the field, I stop and pocket my hands against the mosquitoes. I've never been in this field at dawn, and the life around me now is astounding: Doves whir from the grain to the trees; a doe and fawn feed slowly across into the timber; turkeys gobble and cluck from their roosts; a mile or so down into the drainage a coyote howls. And from the timber directly across from me, an elk chirps, sharp and loud.

The wind has turned. Until it turns again, I'll stand and wait, seeing what the elk have in mind.

There is virtue in patience, in the same way that some plants in Appalachia are said to have virtue for taking off warts or averting the evil eye. Patience is the first relic of magic taken into the wilderness.

I wait for another fifteen minutes before deciding to circle on around into that patch of timber.

The doe and fawn fed into this same cover without having seen me—aware of being hunted even while unaware of the hunter. But even they have disappeared. There's nothing in the timber now but a series of empty, eroded holes.

A Quiet Place of Violence

An elk's tracks follow a path around the scalloped rim, traveling steady. This one will let nothing catch up to him. Early in the season, the young bulls do nothing but travel, hoping to find a place to fit in.

That about does it until this evening.

I look at my watch. It's somehow jumped past eight o'clock.

Hunting alone, hunting in this atmosphere of silence and released ego, it is possible to experience time as accumulation rather than dissipation, each gathered moment a measure of your success.

Epiphany

The weather has swung back around its lodestone, raising the temperature enough to ruin elk hunting. When it's hot like this, in the low nineties, the bulls give up on their bugling to laze under a tree in some nice, cool honeyhole. To have a chance at finding an elk, it will have to be forty degrees cooler. Still, that may be tomorrow.

But for now, antelope hunting.

In a dry year, you can bow hunt antelope from waterhole stands. In a wet year, however, with pockets of water standing in every tire track, your best hope is to decoy.

I made my decoy last year, cutting an antelope's lifesized profile out of a sheet of plywood and stretching a real skin across its front. On the back, I fixed a handle and a metal rod to press into the ground. The horns and eyes I left bare, painting them black.

I drive to the base of a long, timbered ridge that cuts between two large fields: a good place to zigzag back and forth under cover.

As I walk, my feet and legs kick up the smell of broken sage; it fills my mouth and my eyes. I'm suddenly walking through every antelope hunt in the world.

Antelope hunters see more action than their elk hunting counterparts. The animals are easily spotted in the middle of their fields, allowing the bulk of the morning to be spent crawling through the sage and cactus. They are one of the easier big game species to kill with a rifle, especially on the first few days of the season, but they can be nearly impossible with a bow: their sharp eyes and the shelter of their space.

The antelope hunter, like all hunters, faces a dilemma. How far can you reduce the technology without reducing the legitimacy of the project? Aristotle was right at least to this extent—mediums have an ethical appeal.

Extremes of technology distract us away from the process. But the project needs to be valid in order to return us to the process. And the ideal medium, I think, varies according to the individual. For me, a decoy is a good compromise.

I spot the first antelope through the trees, a white spot moving across the field—picking 'em up and setting 'em down. Before I can move the decoy into sight, he's gone.

The second and third antelope are seen together—two small bucks by their black faces—also traveling. They spot me before I can set up the decoy, and hang up about four hundred yards out. From under the neck, I watch them stamp and blow and move around their back legs like pivots. After ten minutes they move on, wheeling across the ridge.

I'm puzzled by those hunters who insist on denying emotions to the animals they hunt. An antelope is so obviously lonely, curious, or fearful, a rutting bull so obviously angry, that emotions are the first thing you want to give them.

I think, perhaps, it's another attempt to justify that which is felt but not known. It's much easier to defend a pre-ethical activity if the other half of that activity holds no possibility for moral agency. With our background of social ethics, if the prey has been denied those characteristics we've traditionally seen as human, it becomes that much easier to deny them any sort of rights.

But of course within the process, it doesn't matter. Fear of death does not change the reality that death is coming. Perhaps then the greatest danger is in denying emotions not to the animal but to yourself.

I spot the fourth buck bedded down, its back toward me. Ahh. I set up just outside the trees, a few hundred yards away, and blow through my mouth like an antelope, hoping to catch his attention. Actually, it's nothing at all like an antelope. But it works to attract his attention.

He stands and quarters toward me, instantly alert. Within a breath he is running to the decoy. Running.

I set my knee down into a patch of prickly pear and jerk it back. It's not much movement, but the buck pulls up about eighty yards out. He blows, using his lower belly like a bellows, sending out a curious trill. It sounds like a startled whitetail backed up by a kazoo.

They are such elegant animals: the well-muscled chest, the thin, veined legs, the slickness of the skin.

A mosquito lands on the back of my hand and takes off again a full minute later: sluggish.

The antelope blows.

His horns are only eleven or twelve inches long, but they're nicely curved, and have good prongs.

The wires between us tremble and pull tight. I see the decoy as he must see it, feeling his puzzlement and fear, his curiosity and fear, his loneliness and fear. I am close enough to see his eyes, to even make out his long, black lashes. And whether I kill him or not, we have this: two parts of one whole.

The wind's picking up. If it's going to happen it will have to be soon.

He takes a step closer and I can see that it's his final step before running. You learn to read these things. He takes off, stopping after a hundred yards for a last look, and then disappears into the trees. I feel myself breathing and it's like I've never breathed before.

I pull up the decoy and walk back to the truck, stopping briefly to pick the cactus spines out of my knee. I'd forgotten they were there.

There are moments when you are unaware of yourself as an individual. And this is what you strive for. This is why the patience.

But none of us are hunting as well as we could be. Our social alienation has diffused into all areas of life, even hunting. Given this, a true hunting ethic would be one that spoke to our role within the process, and tried to replace us within it.

If nature is a process, then what is hunting?

The action that returns you to the process.

So many things fit together so well. I find myself amazed.

For hunting to be justified, nature must have a deontological worth that precedes the concerns of utilitarianism. And it does. How could we ever look at an antelope buck and ask, because it is unbranded or untagged, what *good* is it? It is complete within itself. It contains its own good.

For hunting to be justified, it must acknowledge this inherent worth. And it does. No ethical hunter has ever approached nature seeking to change it or alter it to his own plans. He has accepted it as it is, as more than enough.

For hunting to be justified, it must itself be a deontological activity. And it is. The self-imposed restrictions behind every hunt acknowledge that the value lies not in the results of the act but in the process of approaching the act. Leopold wrote, "Hunting for sport is an improvement over hunting for food, in that there has been added to the test of skill an ethical code."

For hunting to be justified, it must return you to the process. And it does. It deobjectifies the animal you are hunting in a manner unavailable to any other project, acknowledging the process as a fluid, changeable form.

But there are degrees of return, just as there are degrees of morality. And this parallel is exact.

We have the project of the hunt, which has been inscribed by instinct, which has in turn been inscribed by the process. And we have an ethics, which has been produced by rationality: We have an obligation to the process that produced us.

Now suddenly the sportsman's codes that had previously only *sensed* the good have a stable base. From here, it's possible to *know* the good.

Experience

*T*he elk have disappeared. Perhaps I pushed them too hard, perhaps I smelled too bad (too human), perhaps these particular fields began disagreeing with them. Who knows. All I know is that it rained a couple of days ago and I haven't seen a fresh track since. These animals have abilities that deny the adjective "dumb," but I don't think levitation is among them.

It has frosted two nights in a row. My tomato plants are shriveling under sheets of plastic, but it will be good for the bugling.

Elk are so substantial, so essential, that the entire landscape often recedes around them. I love these animals. If you hunt long enough, well enough, striving for a succession of days or years to see the world through the eyes of your prey, you eventually learn to identify with them. Elk call for the most supreme efforts from the hunter, the most extreme levels of identification, and so are loved *extremely. Trophy deer and antelope tend to inspire the same emotions, but these are variations on a more common species and don't immediately beat the heart like even a cow elk.*

But these around here have disappeared, and now it gets much harder.

I'm a mile down from the main road, following a fence on the western border. There's not much light, so it's slow going, and maybe not the smartest move in the world; you can push them out like this.

It's going to be a long day. If I make the circle I'm planning, I should get back to the cabin around two or three in the afternoon, and then I'll have to walk the road back to get the truck. I packed a lunch: lettuce, tomato, mayo, and elk loin.

I'm thinking of the importance of experience. It's the key to everything. I love the elk ahead of me and know that I love it only because I have experienced other elk, other kills. This has been called the great paradox of the hunt—that we are able to love the animal even while intending to kill it. Instead, I see it as the great verification. How could it be possible to love an animal you had not directly experienced, directly interacted with, species to species, role to role?

It's curious and not especially pretty that for all of our available intellect, humanity has been guided only rarely by reason. The need for a social ethic has been a given largely because of its emotional appeal. One of the chief functions of society is to accord comfort and security to its members. It appeals to us emotionally. In fact social ethics are almost impossible to keep from instituting; anarchy is something only to paint on walls. It has no hold on reality. Fascism, on the other hand—pure control—has always been a temptation.

Darwin himself, following the eighteenth-century philosopher David Hume, assumed that morality is based not so much on reason as on feelings, on experience. He devoted a large part of *The Descent of Man* to showing how a moral sense could have evolved, arguing that those social groups which had been selected out for social emotions (such as sympathy) would have outcompeted those groups with less social emotion.

I'm glad I'm following this fence before the weather turns too cold. I've seen all this country in scattered chunks, from different vantages, but never in one continuous strip. Other than the squared, conspicuous butte behind me, this chunk of the Breaks has a distant sameness that requires you to get down into it.

I dip through a small fold of land and find myself on the rim of a deep hole, barely sensing the bottom in this dim light.

Where a road has the luxury of curving with the land, sweeping along ridges in graceful arcs, a border fence juts back and forth in pure geometry: straight ahead and damn the landscape. This love for corners is an inheritance from the militaristic Romans, with their Italian hills rounded like Rubens's women. They should have built fence in the Breaks.

The problem is that an ethic of nature appeals to us rationally but not emotionally. We must be made to *feel* the necessity—the hole in the sky that burns cancer into your skin, the destruction of an ecosystem, the importance of the hunt, the tragedy of its potential loss. If the entire world could spend a weekend out hunting, then perhaps it would be possible to create an environmental ethic with some solvency.

It's darker down in the hole, even as the sun rises. I could have walked back up and around it, but I do have a sense for the melodramatic completion of projects. I set out to walk this fence and by God....

At one end, and in the dimness, I can see the vague shape of a bowl scooped out under a small sandstone wall. Beneath the hanging ledge of it, the darkness swirls like the colors behind your eye. The fence jumps across the hole; a log wired to the bottom strand dangles down low, providing a barrier to livestock.

I crest the small ridge and look into Hay Coulee. Just a few miles south and east, next to the cabin, this drainage is barely enough to support a few cottonwoods, but down here it's a canyon.

I take a seat just below the crest and slide out of my pack frame. The wind is so still: I could hear, or be heard, for miles. A good time to sit and hope for a bugle.

The value of stillness is constantly impressed upon good hunters. We live surrounded by noise, by computers and car alarms, Randy Travis and Rachmaninoff, and when the noise abates, even for a few minutes, we find it unusual. But this should be the constant. Not utter silence, just...quiet. Room for other, unexpected noises. Room to hear the approach of predators, or be heard.

Bishop Berkely famously wrote, *esse est percipi* (to be is to be perceived), meaning that that which isn't perceived doesn't exist. If this idea holds no rational truth, it certainly holds a nearly absolute emotional truth. While

A Quiet Place of Violence

Berkely was radical in saying that objects need an observer to create them, it's not so radical to say that emotional truths, triggered by experience, twist the gut to a greater degree than rational truths. We might realize rationally that a million people are homeless in this country, but feel no urge to do anything about it until we tour a few shelters, work in a few soup kitchens. CNN can tell us that ten thousand people died in a Chinese earthquake, but unless we were there to dig through the rubble for survivors, it's just another fact to eventually forget along with the day's baseball scores.

For an ethic of nature to be applicable, nature must be experienced. And since nature resides in the relationship of animals to one another and to their environment in the roles of original intention, we must hunt. We must stare into the face of our prey as it stares into ours, crazed with blood and snow and the sound of our matched breaths.

We must cultivate a felt need in order to understand the pushes and pulls of the process.

The sun is melting the frost. Before the new moisture can soak through my jeans, I stand and walk a few steps down the hill, past the sun, to stand next to a leaning pine tree. Its roots have pulled out of the ground on the uphill side. Next to it, the trunk of a smaller tree has elbowed at the base—evidence of a slow slip. Odd. Usually surface erosion does them in, not slips. Then I notice how the ridge is terraced, and how the upper level has funneled moisture down below the surface.

I promised myself before setting out this morning that I wouldn't bugle. I just wanted to listen. It's still too early, too hot during the day. But it's so quiet, and there's so much space in front of me.

To bugle, you press your tongue against the three layers of rubber, the reed, and force your breath through between tongue and reed. The harder you press, the higher the note. It should begin as a low, bassy growl, rise over two-to-five tiers, and then fall rapidly after five seconds or so. By general rule, the fewer the tiers, the younger the bull—although this doesn't always hold true. It generally seems better to imitate a younger bull than an older one—to keep from intimidating the competition.

I pull the end of the tube around from over my back and put the reed in my mouth, moistening it and pressing it finally against my palate and teeth.

The call echoes back from the other side of the drainage and fades.

I wait ten minutes. Then fifteen. The sun moves. Every bow hunter has a story about the bull who snuck up on him from behind without making a sound. "Without a sound," they say, shaking their heads.

It almost sounds ridiculous—that you should have to hunt in order to believe an ethic of nature. But consider it through a process of elimination. For the photographer, any ethic that preserved his vista or tamed his animals would work, since these are the aspects of nature that he values and has experienced. For the hiker or the rock climber, any ethic that kept the peaks free of people and the valleys clear of factories would be fine. And even for a devoted naturalist, the order is only something to quantify and objectify, to remove himself from. Scientific observation is still only observation. So long as the data keeps coming in, certain levels of disruption are permissible.

Only for the hunter or gatherer is the process anything other than something apart. And only for the hunter or gatherer must the process be maintained in its most complete state. Only then can his or her project be completely fulfilled. Only then can the natural world be entirely loved.

It's so evident that a hunter's love for the animal follows the act of hunting rather than precedes it. How could anyone love an animal without having experienced it, having interacted with it? You see a baby seal on a poster, and its large eyes, soft, white fur, and nearly human face immediately recommend it for a large dose of sympathy. But how is this love? How could you love an animal without knowing the way it fulfills its role, the way it reacts to a predator, and most importantly, the way *you* react to it? How could you love an animal through any role that objectified it, that placed you at a distance from it?

Love for the animal you're hunting is found in the meeting of project and process. Your project appropriates the animal as an extension of yourself: thus the love. But the process teaches you the lack of adequate definition for Self, allowing the animal to appropriate *you*: thus the love. Without experience, what you are loving is the *idea* of the animal, not the animal itself.

Philosophical empiricism believes that all of knowledge, all of what Hume called, "matters of fact and real existence," must be based upon experience. If you accept this argument, is it a surprise that the demographic group that has most experienced the wilderness in a posture of respect also has the deepest roots in conservation?

The hunter's promotion of conservation can be traced to the 1870s, when it arose as a reaction against market hunting and habitat destruction. This was over thirty years before the word "conservation" even entered the popular vocabulary. The subtitle of *Forest and Stream*, first published in 1873, read: "A Weekly Journal Devoted to Field and Aquatic Sports, Practical Natural History, Fish Culture, The Protection of Game, Preservation of Forests and the Inculcation in Men and Women of a Healthy Interest in Outdoor Recreation and Study."

Theodore Roosevelt and Gifford Pinchot, both hunters, were directly responsible for setting aside 150 million acres in National Forests, five National Parks, and fifty-three National Wildlife Refuges. George Bird Grinnell, historically the most important editor of *Forest and Stream*, was instrumental in creating Glacier National Park. The Pittman-Robertson Act, which imposes an 11 percent excise tax on firearms and ammunition, has purchased at least four million acres for conservation; duck stamps, another four million; various hunter conservation groups (like The Rocky Mountain Elk Foundation and Foundation for North American Wild Sheep), three million; and state hunting licenses, five million. (It's noteworthy that these are the opposition's own numbers and that the reality is probably higher.) FNAWS has directly contributed almost twenty million dollars to causes benefitting wild sheep.

This is all old news. And it has too often been mustered in support of the wrong arguments. A strong history in conservation is not enough, in itself, to justify hunting. Hunters have done a great deal more to preserve and defend the environment than their opposition, but for the animal rights activists, such a history fails to speak to the pain being caused the animals, which is their primary concern. Neither does it speak to *why* hunters hunt.

Well, hunters provide conservation funds, hunters balance wildlife populations, and provide wildlife professionals with information that can only be obtained through examination of large samples of animals. But for that well-intentioned individual who sees animals on a par with humans, economics is not a justification. And balancing wildlife populations? Different groups have worked to "tie the tubes" of deer in the overpopulated East rather than shoot them. And there is very little statistical information that could not be obtained through methods such as photography, aerial studies, and darting.

Why do people hunt? Because if we're going to relate to the natural world in our evolved role, we *must* hunt. Otherwise, nature exists as an object to be exploited. The other benefits of hunting may serve a purpose, but they're incidental.

Our history in conservation should be used as *evidence* of inclusion and love for the process. By their acts, hunters have realized the value of the natural world. Their willingness to fight for its preservation has come as a natural extension of this realization.

Conservation is not why we hunt. We hunt because it's our role within the process. But we have realized the value of the process through the act of hunting and, having realized the value, have fought to preserve it.

The sun has reached me again. I walk to the bottom of the hill and up the other side, feeling how firm the still frosty ground is, how it supports my weight.

Our ethical obligation is finally to health: the health of the process and the larger spirals of which we are a part. How we reach that health is the nexus of the debate.

Respect

There's something essential about walking. A good walk recalls our origins. A few Stone Ages ago, as environmental conditions forced our various prey species into migration, we followed them or we starved. We sang our way "across the wilderness," as Bruce Chatwin put it.

Some of our most illustrious singers have been walkers. To compose his poetry, Wallace Stevens was known to walk thirty or forty miles a day. One of Rimbaud's companions said of him that he had foot soles of wind. It's even possible that the meter of Dante's Divine Comedy, humanity's greatest verse accomplishment, is meant to mimic the rhythm of walking. Our singers walked, as did our teachers, as did our iconoclasts. Jesus walked through his holy land and Buddha compared the way of

A Quiet Place of Violence

enlightenment to "*a path to be and to be walked upon.*" Camus, Kierkegaard, and Nietzsche were also great walkers, walking into the essential.

For now, I walk my fence. The blisters on my heels are still sensitive, and the ball of one toe seems bruised, but I feel good.

As the sun warms the ground, a column of mosquitoes twists up through the light in the coulee, moving with a single mind. The tenacity of these things. They trace, within the spiral of their flight, the same mathematical curve found in some sea shells, the whirl of hair on a balding man's head, the spin of draining water, and the shape of our own galaxy: Fibonacci's series, it's called. Numerically, it holds to the pattern 1, 2, 3, 5, 8, 13...wherein the next number in the series is a product of the previous two. That is, if one rotation is five inches wide, the sections on either side of it will be three and eight inches.

We name it, this series, but we don't understand it. With all of our scientific knowledge, all our observation of the manifestations of being, we still can't imagine what it means. We know that death has pulled a palate of infinite color from the first living cells, but we don't know why. Why would two hundred species of mosquito be more significant than one? How is a black cottonwood more important than a sheet of blue algae? Why would nature go to all the trouble to create the Breaks if it is only going to turn around and erode them away? The world's inflated with its own sense of fecundity and purpose—but all to no good, apparent end. And if we don't understand it, how could we possibly presume to change it—or worse, appropriate it?

Respect is all that we can hope to fully accomplish.

When you kill a fly, say a little prayer over it. You've

taken a life and changed the world. When you kill a fly, realize yourself as fly swatter and world changer, and then go back to washing the dishes with a fuller realization of yourself. If you choose not to kill it, say a little prayer, for you have changed the world.

I start walking up out of the coulee. The first shoulder of ridge is thick with tall grass. The sight recalls certain high mountain pastures. As much as the Breaks are home, I still miss mountain sunrises.

R espect accompanies our role.

As predators, we have an ethical obligation to eat what we kill—ethical since not eating it would be beyond the original intention of hunting. If nothing else, the life of the process is dependent upon the free exchange of energy among its members.

And so we've been taught that it's disrespectful to waste the animal you have killed.

I sit below the crest of a gumbo bank and rest my elbows on my knees, holding the binoculars. It's still early—I could catch sight of an elk as it moves into bed. I focus on the furthest point of the horizon, the long ridge of Squaw Creek, but...nothing. I focus on the next closest ridge. Still, nothing. Then on the ridge just across, with its rows of shoulders. And I catch a glimpse of movement.

Deer, running. About a dozen does and fawns are already disappearing into the timber. Two large does linger back, staring with tense, straight legs down into the drainage. It's a posture I know well.

And so I expect another hunter to come up from below. Instead, I watch a pair of white backs slink—this is the word, slink—across one of the small ridges. Coyotes.

A Quiet Place of Violence

Even from this distance, I can make out the sharp slope of their faces, and the way they cast their noses back and forth as they trot and stop, trot and stop. These are also postures I know well. Predation requires a level of attention necessarily greater than the prey.

The coyotes move out of sight and, after a moment, I move on myself, up the next small ridge to glass further into the coulee. And before I even have a chance to sit down, I see a pair of slowly moving brown spots that can only be elk. The binoculars make them out to be a cow and a calf. As I watch, a spike comes up on them from behind.

They are almost a mile away, feeding across the crest of the drainage into a patch of juniper and pine.

If I were to go into that thicket from the opposite end, breaking branches with my imaginary antlers and chirping like a cow, I might call in the big bull that is undoubtedly hanging around just out of sight.

At the bottom of the ridge, looking up into the stand of juniper that has become the horizon, I bugle. Ostensibly, I do it to place the elk, but I really do it because I enjoy bugling so much. That is, I enjoy having my bugle answered so much.

And within a minute, I'm answered by a short, high-pitched squeal from the furthest edge of the brush; about where I'd expected.

My stomach flutters and I charge up the hill, making as much noise as possible. Once in the thicket I break brush and dig at the ground with my heels; they already think I'm an elk, so it's best to play it up. Finally, I break off a branch from a dead tree and run it up and down the trunk, rattling it around in the limbs.

I wait, hoping to hear the same thing from the other end, but there's only an obstinate, perhaps surprised, silence.

Slinking now, I work my way around the thicket on the uphill side, hoping to intercept the bull.

But...nothing. I stop and listen, looking down toward the jungle-dark thicket. I step into it, hoping against what I know that the elk might be coming toward me. I bugle again, and after a few minutes the spike squeals from the other side of the hill.

They've gone out ahead of me. At least they're going deeper into the ranch.

The problem is, bugling is too much fun. My brother, who is a better hunter than I am, would have tried to quietly ambush them as they bedded down. His project is more authentic: He's hunting to make the kill. My project is usually tainted by enjoyment of certain aspects of the hunt not directly related to its fulfillment: the walking, the bugling, the watching. I spend too much time aware of myself as a hunter.

The elk followed the same ridge into the ranch that I had planned on taking. Rather than pushing them, I decide to turn back to the truck. It won't be such a long day after all.

I was thinking of respect.

If the world is a system, and a system based on change, then its groundwork is the unimpeded relationships between its members and their environment: they live and die, eat and are eaten.

The most accessible kind of respect arises from this obvious kind of reciprocation. I hunt and kill and eat an elk, and in this way become a member of the process.

But aren't there other possible attitudes of respect that don't rely on ecology? What can I more subtly accept and what can I return?

Everything. Nothing. Nothing less than all it asks, all I need.

Modern environmental writers seem unusually fond of grocery lists, trying to prove through bulk all the benefits of wilderness. There's the aesthetic, they say, the spiritual, the financial, the medicinal, the psychological, the genetic. But their lists all end with the idea that wilderness should be valued apart from all this, respected for its own dignity. They are right, of course, but not precisely.

In 1859, as part of his own Copernican revolution, Darwin removed humanity from the center of the universe. He forced us to see our own species as changeable, and therefore as un-unique, as all of the other little live things on earth. At the turn of the century, Freud published his *Interpretation of Dreams* to a cool response that heated into an explosion. Part of Freud's doctrine was the idea that mental illness came as a result of animality being repressed by civilization. In 1910 Einstein told us that time, space, and size are all relative.

For most of us, the greatest value of the wilderness lies in its offered stability, usually sensed only as potential. And for the best of us, the quietest of us, this potential can be realized. We can find an identity based on that which has no identity: a part among parts.

I could *be* nature.

It's only then that we might be able to fully reciprocate, seeing in the process a dignity beyond our own egos. Without this sense of belonging, all arguments for the inherent worth of wilderness are lip service to a neat idea.

Intrinsic worth can only be seen from the inside. My country is valuable enough to fight for only because I am a part of it. A little girl's doll is worth something only because she has placed an aspect of herself onto it—it's *her* doll. So long as there is an Other from which to take or give, the Other's inherent worth is in doubt. If nature is perceived as an Other, then we are always going to be the ones that are the more valuable, if only as the subjects that perceive an object.

I walk along a small, timbered section of fence I had earlier skipped, and come upon the skeleton of an antelope buck hanging by its front leg, twisted between the top two strands of wire.

It's rare for an antelope to try and jump a fence. They almost always slide beneath. In the hardest winters, great numbers of them will drift with the wind until, if they hit a sheep fence, they will die in piles. But every now and then one will take a chance.

Dry skin hangs in permanent folds against his bare bones, turning slowly into humus. The back legs and ribs have been scattered by coyotes, but a front shoulder, three neck vertebrae, and the skull all hang intact above the ground.

I can't budge the wires—they're wound that tight. I finally break the leg in two and beat the hoof and foreleg on through the wire. The shoulder thumps to the ground, but the horns hook on the bottom wire, swinging the skull lightly back and forth.

I leave them, the elation from bugling having been replaced by a sense of sadness and isolation.

That was my *fence.*

STABILITY

*S*tars and falling snow, running water and fire: each draws the eye, each promotes its own brand of melancholy.

The first snow fell last night. It began shortly before dark, when the ground was still warm from the day's sun, and lasted only long enough to skim the roof of my cabin. It was snow as the material changing of a season. The world has been a certain way for the past four months, and in the space of several hours it changed completely. The low, pervasive voice under the soil—the single note that I have been hearing for weeks now—seemed somehow muffled.

I woke this morning to find the fields streaked with frosty mud. The wet boots set out to dry yesterday afternoon were frozen blocks, and the empty tomato plants were shriveled carcasses. Above the house, yearling steers

lie away from the wind in rings around the hills.
Respect feels like it's unfinished.

First in the spiral of respected things must be yourself. Above all else, the hunter must hunt through the process. He must be dignified.

Coming back from dinner at the neighbors, you swing your headlights through the lawn and startle a thirty-four-inch buck, blinding him. Your first impulse, regardless of personal ethics, is to jump out and shoot it. Your whole life this is what you've been hunting for. And here it is. Right in front of you.

But to kill that animal would be to let project take precedent over process. It would be unnatural, unethical. There would be no stalk, no moment of accord between the hunter and the animal, no real chance for it to escape—everything would exist beyond the process. You might kill the buck, but by doing so you would have rejected the process of which the deer was a part—of which you were trying to become a part. The act would have been one of pure killing. Not hunting.

You never stop being a predator, regardless of the place or time. This is both a virtue and a danger.

The idea of honor sounds antiquated these days, more suited to an age of steel swords than scientific relativism. Honor distilled is nothing less than self-respect, and self-respect has lately been taking a bad rap. Is it too fortuitous to think that a need for an ethics based on respect comes at a time when respect itself has become a valueless commodity?

It must be possible to restore those virtues which a modern condition has found superfluous and restricting.

A Quiet Place of Violence

Honor. Dignity. Courtesy.

Any document of ethics must at the same time be a document of virtues.

From this, I'm going on to gopher shooting. It all fits.

As a nine year old near Philipsburg, I once killed 796 gophers with a new .22. One of the problems—if we are predatory animals, and if nature is predicated upon violence and death—is control. Why not kill as much as we like?

Freud had a few things right. We have our basic instincts, our basic drives, and if we're screwed up, it is due in part to the suppressions of society. Just watch a little boy with his first BB gun, shooting bluebirds off the line, shooting the neighbor's dog, shooting anything. This is what we are before rationality controls us.

In a summer, I shot 796 gophers. But now I swerve to miss them. In an afternoon I once shot two successive doubles on doves and still see it as an accomplishment. Is there a difference?

Process! The process. And the ethics of intention.

Through great numbers, the individual can be objectified. It is easier, in many ways, to kill 796 gophers than to kill one alone. The crowd is always an object. The horde around the Pope, as he waves his way through to the podium, contains no hopes or aspirations of its own, no definable identity—it is a crowd, and the individuals within it have been lost to its larger character. Several thousand of us together are capable of tearing Rome apart, of shooting students at Kent State, starting a revolution, but an individual can find it hard to spank her child.

Killing a large number of animals causes a loss of accord between you and the process. If I had stalked each of those gophers on my stomach, if I had skinned and eaten each one, then I could have ethically killed as many as possible. There would have been a dozen or so.

We are individuals. If we hunt, we must hunt other individuals.

If my intention is to return myself to the process, then killing large numbers of animals is counterproductive; it kicks the legs out from under my larger goal. Every prey individual must be hunted according to its role in the process. It's a matter of respect. Accordingly, every predator must hunt according to *its* role. It's a matter of self-respect. Together, these forms of dignity embody ethical hunting; it's a way of acknowledging and respecting the original intention: bloody ablutions to a larger cause.

In this nice way, the ethical blends with the spiritual.

It's dark and snowing again. I had begun to believe that the days were only recycling themselves, like sheets through a machine, but now it turns out that there has been a progression after all.

Tomorrow morning should be the best elk hunting of the season. I'll hunt all day, losing myself in the new snow; it will soften my footsteps, allow me to bend branches rather than break them, and will probably be accompanied by a lapse in the wind. For the first time this year, I will hunt silent and scentless.

Possession

*H*unting requires optimism. *You get up at five o'clock, walk until eleven, rest, and hunt again until dark only because this next hunt is* the one.

I walk from the house on a path I have already traveled four or five times this season. I'll be walking around beneath the grain fields through the Breaks in order to come up onto the flat fields from the unexpected below.

These early snows always make it look like it should be a lot colder than it is. A light skiff erases surfaces but without covering the edges, and the horizontal arrangement gives the world a tough cast.

I bugle below the first field, staring up at the scalloped horizon, and am met with silence. After a few minutes, I move further along, just below the next set of fields, and bugle again. Immediately there's a deep response, and then two high ones from the satellite bulls. They're not close, but they're there.

Genetic or associational, can there be any greater feeling of anticipation than in the first moments of a stalk? Your eyes are bulging with sudden adrenaline and you find yourself taking note of the slightest currents of wind, the smallest movements in the brush, the most incidental flights of birds. All this even while your conscious attention is focused on the animal in front of you. You are awake.

A smaller bull bugles again, perhaps a little further away. I pick up my speed.

The snow has started to melt, and by the time I reach the base of the hill below the field, I'm walking on layered stilts of gumbo and snow. I stand to scrape the clods off and look up to see a small five point bull craning its head down at me.

I freeze, holding my breath to small pulses.

Five minutes later the bull grows impatient, disappearing back into the timber, toward herd.

Nothing to do but play it through.

In the trees I bugle again. I hope to keep the bull from spooking and to fix the positions of the other elk. Somehow, there is an answer. And then several answers—all above me and still in the field.

Hunting alone, the nature of possible scenarios changes dramatically. Last year with my father, a bull hung up seventy or eighty yards out and began circling us for our scent. I backed away, breaking limbs and grunting. Dad stayed ahead, positioned behind a juniper bush. The bull was encouraged enough by my retreat to come on in, spooking only as Dad rattled his arrow across a branch.

A Quiet Place of Violence

But alone, with no bugler to distract the bull, quiet stalking is often the best.

If you are hunting well, the state of inclusion perpetuates itself. To fulfill your project, you need to know the land, what forms it takes, and how you can work with them. To kill your bull, you need to know the animal, his habits, and his capacity to avoid you. Most importantly, you need to know yourself, how far you can reasonably walk in a day, how quietly you can stalk. Some hunters announce themselves with trumpets while a very few can slip through the woods in their suits of rustling leaves and trickling water.

If I could move around in front, below them, I might be able to lay an ambush from a narrow finger of timber that I know is there, connecting the field to the ravine.

I scrabble along the sidehill for a half mile before topping out into the string of timber.

The herd is already spread out in the open, not as close to the timber as I had hoped, and still over a hundred yards away. A few of the cows are looking in my direction, ears alert. A few more stand in the timber. I freeze. At the end of the line, a good six point, larger than the earlier bull, stretches his nose out to a cow.

There's no way I can make it around to another ambush without attracting attention. I try a cow call. Twenty heads and a pair of antlers swivel toward me. The cows stand still and the bull steps back and forth, his fight-or-flight impulse triggered. Should he run away? Or should he chase after me?

There is movement off to my left. Two bulls that I hadn't seen, a raghorn and the five point, stand at the edge of the timber on my side, less than seventy yards away. I ease to the side and put a small tree between us, hoping the herd won't spook at my movement.

Cow call again. I lift my bow and prepare to draw, the broadhead trembling across the rest. I hear heavy steps in the wet grass, and smell the elks' musky odor. The raghorn steps out fifteen yards away, staring directly at me. His nostrils quiver. I wait. I can't breathe. I can hear the five point walking up close behind him. He steps between me and the raghorn. Ten yards away, no more. After a few seconds, a few hours, they both turn to look at the herd on the other side of the field. I draw and shoot.

And I die a little as the arrow goes in high. Sometimes the very short distances can be harder than the very long.

But the despair turns into elation as I watch the five point stumble as he runs into the timber. The brush crashes.

The elation dilutes to sadness: Success, but failure.

I sit down where I am. My trembling hands move like flags over my face, over the ground, finally into my pockets.

A badly wounded elk, if it doesn't die immediately, will usually go only a short distance before lying down, sick. If given enough time, maybe just a few minutes, it will die there. If it's forced to keep walking, it can walk its wounds away. I expect to find this one lying just inside the trees. But I've been wrong before.

I'm confident that crash came when he fell. Almost confident. I stand and walk through the field to the timber on the other side.

Twenty feet within the timber, where the steep banks cut into the sun and the temperature drops until I can see my breath, I find the arrow unbroken on an open patch of needles. Thirty feet further on I see an antler curving up out of a deadfall.

I wish there were someone with me, someone else looking, so I could holler back that I've found him and that he's a good one—just to holler. I do it anyway; it feels wrong not to.

Caught in the brush, the antlers twist his head back as if he were just now getting ready to bugle.

I find a place on the dead log slightly above him and sit down, grabbing the antler between the third and fourth points. Solid. Cool.

His legs stretch out in mid stride, black enough to carry a reflection. That's what's made some of the tracks I've been seeing. The thick, knotted hair across his stomach stinks of mud and urine.

Hunting is not an attempt to take possession of the animal, as so many hunters have argued. If that were the case, the attempt is doomed to failure.

I cannot possess the elk. It's dead. But I can possess the memory of it in the moment before I killed it, which is enough. It's more than enough. What I have brought away is my relationship to the animal, not the animal itself.

It is not so much a desire to possess as to be possessed.

And to be possessed, you must hunt him. To hunt him, you must kill him. The words of this hard verity are etched arrow deep into every sandstone bluff, screamed by every dying rabbit, whispered against the cheek of every hunter. We fight for our right to live, marking out our territory in a spray of blood, reddening our teeth and nails on life's hard truths.

And in front of me now, arrested, lies a dead mass of

energy. But it is dead only until it flows back into the process: through me.

Its stomach faces the downhill side. Good luck.

I take off my pack and jacket, roll up my sleeves, break off a few branches to clear the way, and open my knife. Alone, with no one to pull back on the rib cage or arrange its legs, this is going to be a messier job than usual.

Beginning in the middle of the stomach, slightly off to one side to avoid the thickest of the hair, I make a small incision with the edge of the blade. A few inches give way and the white paunch presses out. I slide my first two fingers down into the incision, placing the knife between them, edge up, and make a single long cut up to its rib cage. The paunch expands, pulled by gravity, and when I go back and cut down into the pelvic area, it spills out: stomach, upper intestine, the first lobes of the liver, the small knot of gallbladder. The rest is obscured by a warm wash of blood that swallows my hands and lower arms.

The arrow went in high, it died almost immediately, there's all this blood...I must have sliced the aorta.

The pancreas, the thick neck of the lower intestine, the hard kidneys, these come out next. I reach blindly back up and cut almost randomly, severing all the connections that I can feel. Two of the four or five scars on my fingers have come from this kind of cutting. The largest portion of viscera, now free, slides out into the dead branches.

The year has been wet enough and the growing season long enough, that his fat lies in chunks everywhere; my hands are greasy.

I reach back and carefully extract the bowel and then the bladder, clamping it shut with my thumb and forefinger. Only then do I move back to the testicles, which can give the meat an unpleasant flavor if left close.

For the sternum, I take out and assemble the small game saw I've been carrying all these weeks. It will let me empty the chest cavity of lungs, heart and esophagus without getting bloody past the elbows: an indulgent nicety.

Another wash of aortal blood.

Blood is heavier than water. A bull like this carries five to six gallons of it. If I were Cree I would drink a few swallows to keep from being disturbed by the sight of it in battle.

Within the chest, the lungs are flaccid and spongy, holding their strong lines of contour even as I cut them apart. Inflated, they have a capacity of six gallons.

The blood has spread from the carcass in an expanding arc, soaking through one of my pants legs, turning it tacky and stiff.

I remove the ten-pound heart, still twitching with its physical memory. If I were Crow, I would set it aside as a gesture of respect. I do it anyway.

It's a distancing mechanism, this knowledge. But you have to go through it, just like you have to read the billboards driving through town. The necessity of killing does not make you any happier about doing it, not after you become conscious of yourself.

To remove the cape, I make a cut from the sternum to the top of the shoulder, then another from the crest of the back to a point between and slightly behind the antlers. This done, I grab the corner at the shoulder and pull it away, cutting. Fat stands in layers above the shoulder.

With the cape hanging lose, I cut and twist the neck vertebrae just below the skull, removing the head and setting it aside. Its eyes fall back into its skull. If I were a Flathead, I would close them.

I cut away the front shoulders and rear hips at the joints, setting them on a plastic bag to be boned later. The straps, loins, and ribs I will have to do here.

I remove the skin and make two cuts along the top ridge of the vertebrae (the knife bouncing along the contours of bone) and then horizontally above the ribs. A cut at the front and back, and the first backstrap is cleanly off. I next saw the largest series of ribs away from the vertebrae, using this new space to get at the internal loins.

The elk, now little more than a backbone and half of a ribcage, is easy to turn over for the other strap and ribs.

I set the four legs and ribs off to one side, covering them with an orange plastic tarp. I tie the head, straps, and loins onto my pack frame. It's heavy, but the cabin's no more than three or four miles away. Once home, I'll be able to drive the truck back to within a hundred yards to pick up the legs and ribs. Truthfully, I wouldn't have to pack out anything. But it's a way of paying dues.

Almost exactly two hours after hearing the first bugle, I begin my hike back to the cabin.

Freedomless

I would like to know without a doubt that killing the elk was praiseworthy. But where death sticks its nose (and its nose goes on forever), there can be no absolute knowledge. Still, I remember the stalk and the moment of the kill and the way I melted into the larger action, and I *feel* to the wick of my soul that the kill was necessary.

You have your reasons and rationalizations, and you know them well, but each dead animal forces you to confront them all over again. Scars do recall the wounds. After enough kills, enough scars, the dialectic forces you to abandon some of the views you began with.

You do not hunt out of blood lust. This is the most essential truth. If you enjoy seeing animals die, you're already so far beyond the intentions of the process as to be nearly irredeemable. No sanity gets a kick out of destroying a life—the blood and viscera and knowledge of endings that come of it.

It may seem ridiculous even to the hunter—that is, intending to do what he doesn't enjoy or perhaps even abhors. But death and blood are the terms we've been given. You hunt so that you may be included in something larger than yourself, something essential and beautiful. And this is an animus that cares nothing for your feelings of abhorrence or reluctance. It's concerned only with aggregates of individuals, not the individuals themselves. Eventually, even what we consider to be ourselves will be eaten and shit out, regardless of how important we just now think we are. In my case, Breaks worms will procreate in my colon, waltz across my bare pelvis, roll dice with my metacarpals.

But physical reunion does not lead to psychological or spiritual reunion, and these are the ethical concerns. We must not kill entirely for the food, since food without experience means nothing. Nor must we kill for the blood, although blood necessarily results. If I am hunting without the intention of spilling blood I am only an observer, watching others play the crucial game while I stand on the sidelines, thinking myself beyond it.

It must always be remembered: There is no beyond. Where death is concerned all freedoms and choices are illusory, a short run on the leash before our necks are snapped back. In this context, a process ethic is somewhat self-negating. If we could ever fully return ourselves to the process, we would have no need for an ethic since we would have no ability to choose our actions.

Ethics limit freedom, but if we were ever to be absolutely included within the natural order—if we could ever be brought to this enviable point—we would have *no* freedom, no choice of action at all.

I walk out on the porch and am surprised to see a thin, silent rain falling, caught as gruel between snow and water. The pile of wood looks soaked, but after taking off the top layer I find a few dry sticks. I stand and gaze around for a moment, rough wood in my hands.

The necessity of limiting freedom and the enjoyment of it contradicts almost everything we've been taught to think of as desirable. Our peculiar canon of virtues has always put Freedom at the top of the list. But it's the price to be paid, this loss of self and self-will: it's the gift. Killing is not enjoyable, but the kill must be made if the hunter is to be sacrificed to the larger order.

You watch it from across the way, its head down, its new blood melting Rorschach patterns in the snow. It falls and you run to it.

Under your hands, its antlers are cold and smooth, and steam from the open wound blends into the cloud of your breath. You inhale the mix: sage and blood and the wildness of sex.

Everything has led up to this union; everything leads away.

The kill is a catalyst, condensing into it all your previous, essential moments. Perhaps it necessitates mindlessness. Perhaps to hunt and kill an animal is to find the point where moral laws collapse in upon themselves.

How could you kill an innocent animal.

This has been a favorite question of almost everyone

who hasn't experienced the hunt. Innocence is a crucial concern. It is what immediately stands out. And it places the burden of proof upon the hunter.

The crux of it is that the deer is not innocent. Innocence implies the possibility for guilt. Innocence implies choice. The coyote is not guilty for eating a deer, and neither is the deer guilty for eating grass. They have no choice about their actions. In the same way, neither of them are innocent. That which is without freedom is without innocence or guilt. It simply *is*.

This idea of innocence fits neatly into the traditional paradox of trying to impose human ideals, human ways of ordering the world, onto an amoral system. The world is neither innocent nor guilty. It is only to humans, with our reserve of rational choices, that these words have been pointed.

How could I kill an innocent deer?

I could not.

How could I kill a deer?

Because I must.

Mercy

*T*he year is passing. Despite all attempts to retain the moment, it rests its heels and bows out. Yesterday was the first day of rifle season, a Sunday, and all day I could hear the hollow reports of gunfire, mostly from the public access at Devil's Creek.

The year passes. I have my elk, have given up on an antelope and have decided to concentrate on deer hunting.

I have in mind that buck I saw on the skyline and the larger buck undoubtedly behind that one. There is always a larger buck, somewhere, at the edge of the timber.

I am standing on the fringe of a CRP field, my breath clouding up my glasses. It's only been a couple of weeks since I was hunting elk and already I feel out of shape.

These are mule deer I'm hunting—slightly less prolific than whitetails and slightly easier to hunt. While a large whitetail buck will ease down into the brush and lower its antlers to watch you pass, its mule deer counterpart, no less aware or sagacious, will be seen more often—if only as it splits for the next county.

Early in the season, you hunt the corrugations, dropping from the back of one ridge to climb the next, hoping to flush the bucks from their beds. The shots you have will be running shots, and the opportunities you have will be impossible for a bow, at least until the last week or two in November.

Despite my various diatribes against technology, for these first two weeks I've rested my bow against the wall and picked up my rifle, a 7mm Remington Magnum. As a concession to this technology, I have also raised my standards. Later on, with my bow, I'll not hesitate to shoot anything over twenty-four inches, but with the rifle I don't intend to kill a buck less than twenty six.

The project must be legitimate. I must feel that I am hunting, not just walking the hills with a useless weapon.

This is largely how I grew up, with a leather strap over one shoulder. And returning to it now gives me a sense of slippage. The sheet separating adult from child is never more substantial than the moment, and this can be pulled away by the smell of a mother's perfume, the rustle of a newspaper, the distended click of a cartridge sliding into the barrel.

It snowed a bit last night; for now, before the sun rises, all the piles of old cow shit are rippled, pretty blooms.

Yesterday, watching the procession of faceless hunters on the public road, I was surprised to feel a kind of church-going jealousy: that's my God, there, bub. Other hunters have too much leg, too little head, to entirely fit in.

It's been argued that rifle hunting is superior to bow

A Quiet Place of Violence

hunting because of its aspects of mercy. Yet, is this a valid concern? Are hunting and mercy exclusive states? Can the hunter be merciful and still hunt? Is he, in fact, cruel?

These are the deep questions, cutting to expose the bones of the thing. The animal rights activists are smug in their answers: the hunter cannot be merciful, yes he is cruel. But there are no absolutes, and the questions remain, forcing the hunter into his seasonal dark nights of the soul.

The engendering emotion behind any merciful act is pity, and pity arises from having seen the world through another set of eyes. That is, if that were to happen to me, this is how I would feel. *His son was killed in a car accident? His* son? *Oh God!*

It's perhaps the foundation of social ethics, empathy. And it's easily displaced. It's so easily displaced, in fact, that animal rights activists always seem to preface their arguments by, "How would you like…?" How would you like to be shot? How would you like to be gutted? How would you like for your head to be hung on a wall?

It's a ridiculous irony. We *will* die, we *will* be put on the universal table, we *are* caught in a trap. Asking how-would-you-like to the natural order assumes that we ourselves, the ones who are asking the question, might somehow be exempt, might escape the death implicit within the order.

Unlike an ethic of society, an ethic of the process does not require putting yourself in someone else's shoes. The shoes are already ours. And they cannot be stepped away from. The *attempts* to step away from them, however, proliferate.

Mercy is essential to society, but it is outside the process. Pity is among our strongest emotions, but if one is going to hunt, it must always, to some degree, be resisted. Just as blood lust is beyond the process, so precisely are pity and mercy. And for the same reason: *intentionality*.

To be merciful, you must first consciously intend it, and conscious intention denies the process.

A friend and I once lay down in a field of old grain, shooting geese as they flew in to our decoys. That morning's hunt was the best either of us had experienced for several years, and we finished the morning with laughter and good feelings. But walking back to the truck, a single goose circled above us, honking for a mate whose neck one of us held. And the good feelings died away.

My brother and a friend once shot the two largest rams from a small herd, and as they skinned them, took photographs and shook hands, the remnants of the herd milled around on a distant shale slide, stepping toward them and falling back. Their leaders were gone, and so they did not know how to behave.

Another friend tells of killing a wolf in Canada and describes his own sadness as the pack followed them into camp that night to howl out their anger and despair behind the tents.

Socially, pity is necessary and good. Within the process, complete mercy only further removes us from the process.

This must be immediately explained.

Mercy is an odd concept in that it tolerates no medium. I am on the streets of Sri Lanka with ten dollars in my pocket and I walk by a crippled child with a bowl in his hands. I am cruel if I realize the child's need and do nothing; I am merciful if I drop the ten dollars in his bowl.

A Quiet Place of Violence

Once I am aware of the child's need, I must be either merciful or cruel. There is no middle ground. My deer is struggling on the ground, its back broken, tongue distended, its eyes rolled back. Cruelty lies in watching it die, mercy in killing it quickly. There is no middle ground. Awareness necessitates action.

Once you know, you can't go back. This is the burden of knowledge.

For an ethic, it is enough to say that inaction with ignorance is innocence. Inaction with knowledge is guilt.

If one is a cruel hunter, that is, if one intentionally allows unnecessary pain to exist, then, at the worst, it is a sign of serious illness and, at the best, one of complete estrangement. As estrangement, the pain is allowed to continue because the animal is seen only as an object, a Cartesian machine. As illness, the animal is seen as sentient creature, and still the pain is allowed to exist, perhaps because the hunter doesn't want to waste a bullet, or because he enjoys pain.

Within our alienation, mercy is necessary because cruelty is abhorrent.

But the ideal state is one in which neither mercy nor cruelty exist, in which conscious intentions have been absorbed by the process. If we were ever to find full replacement, mercy would be a nonissue. The process precedes mercy and cruelty. A coyote can be neither merciful nor cruel given that it is acting without awareness or intention. But since we always retain some level of consciousness, since we have the ability to be self-aware, no one, not even the worst of us, is utterly untouched by a goose circling, a wolf howling. The danger lies in letting this pity preclude the process.

In the same way that one shouldn't let project take precedence over process (killing the animal at all costs), one should also not let mercy take precedence over process (not killing at all). In their extremes, both conditions alienate.

A popular argument in favor of hunting has been that since it is impossible to live an entirely non animal-abusive existence, it is probably better to admit your limitations and, if not go hunting, at least sanction it as inevitable. You mean you hate hunting, but you wear leather shoes?

But this argument is already looking in the wrong direction in that it assumes hunting to be cruel and abusive. It is not.

An ethical hunter, one who is hunting to fulfill a role within the process, does not *intend* abuse. Rather, as has been said, he is hunting *in spite of* the necessary abuse.

For the complete hunter, mercy would no longer be an issue since his acts would exist without intention.

Unfortunately, none of us stand completely within the process. Perhaps full inclusion is impossible. Mercy will always be an issue since there will always be some level of intention behind the hunt. In the hours or days between stalks, when we are aware of ourselves as individuals, when we are capable of intention, then mercy and cruelty reenter the world as virtue and vice.

Elective incompetence is, in many ways, the worst of cruelties. It represents a disregard both for the animal you're hunting as well as your own responsibili-

A Quiet Place of Violence

ties as a predator. If you feel uncomfortable making a two-hundred-yard shot, limit yourself to one-hundred-yard shots, and adjust your expectations accordingly.

I've really got to cut out all this mind crap. When I should be losing myself in the hunt, I'm losing myself in the issues—a much uglier place.

The wind blows cold dust from my tracks up into my face; as I walk, I taste raw pottery.

I continue the circle, paying less attention to the wind given the rifle in my hands. I pass the CRP fields and come up on an old alfalfa patch, greened here and there by a volunteer crop. This late in the season, green is again attractive, and I spook out a group of twenty or so antelope. I haven't seen this many antelope together all year.

On the other edge of the field stand three small mule deer bucks—a three point and two forked horns. They spook with the antelope, bouncing down into the timber.

I follow each with my scope, taking the shallow, controlled breaths that steady the barrel—physically intending to kill them long before I'm consciously aware of it. If any of these animals could fulfill my project I would shoot it immediately, not wasting a moment to stop and consider the rightness of it.

Despite my dedication to and enjoyment of the bow, there is no question that the project of rifle hunting is more legitimate in its feeling of sure success. It's easier. But perhaps it's harder to reach the greater purpose, which is inclusion in the process.

Still, eventually, things begin to happen. First you feel comfortable with the woods, your weapon, yourself, and then you begin forgetting that there was ever any distinction between them at all.

Controls

Someone has decided that now should be the time for migrations, and so the sky has lately been filled with exotic transients.

A group of a dozen or so magpies passed through the yard last week, long tails hanging down and the white on their shoulders flashing. The next day, a number of crows flew across the hills above the house, yelling back and forth like adolescents. There was also a peregrine falcon on the main road, flying beside my truck and dipping away.

And this:

Walking up one of the short ridges of Lost Creek, I startled a hawk away from its perch on the horizon. It was almost as large as a red-tailed hawk, but with a black-and-white angular pattern on the underside of its wings. It was the first rough-legged hawk I've seen in the

A Quiet Place of Violence

Breaks this year. I followed it with my binoculars, enthralled by a new bird in such an old sky. When I pulled my eyes away, a sudden, swirling mass of rough-legged hawks punched me back on my heels: thirty-three birds gliding in thirty-three separate epicycles, a compounded mass of rings. Richness!

I have never seen this before. I might never again. But some new potential has now been added to the Breaks.

I would like to hunt and eat hawks, to have myself appropriated by the fusion of strength and delicacy found in the jerk of their heads, the spurs of their eyes. But my first obligation is to the process, and this obligation means not killing most other predators, particularly birds of prey. In its constancy, their role is more essential to population stability and systems health than my own, which can be fickle and inconsistent.

I once killed a mountain lion. And I did feel the process behind the hunt (despite the intrusion of the dogs), and we did eat all of the cat that was edible (the best meat ever), but I still felt awkward in the act. In retrospect, it didn't seem part of the original intention—to have such knowledge and intensity reduced to the span of a scope. I ended by thinking, I shouldn't have done this.

It would be impossible to say that killing predators is unnatural or unethical. As part of the frenzied tarantella we're all dancing, our most remote ancestors undoubtedly killed what they could. But each of us must make our separate kinds of peace, and I am too aware of myself as an intrusion when I kill other large predators.

For another hunter, predator hunting might be just the thing to push him or her over into full inclusion. It is difficult not to see the predators as competition, not to use undue amounts of technology to kill them, not to use their fur for financial gain, but if it's done well, the trees will bow and the seraphim will applaud.

Above all, hunting must not disrupt that order to which it belongs.

If hunting can be defined as that action which returns you to the process, then most acts of animal killing are unjustified.

To kill large numbers is unethical. To kill for blood lust is unethical. To kill with excessive technology is unethical. This has been decided.

And so population control, particularly predator control, is a problem.

If your project is to control populations, then the animal being killed has become a means to another end: an object. The difference is one of intention. If I am killing predators, my only intention is to make the kill to control the population. If I am hunting, my intention is to become part of the process. The first objectifies the animal as something to be manipulated, the second places the animal on a plane parallel with the hunter. In order to save some grass, you shoot prairie dogs, seeing them only as terms of a function. Ideally, hunting and its deobjectification would suffice, and there would be no need for population control, but in our current situation, population control that is not hunting is often an ecological necessity.

This is where it gets sticky. The whole thing.

We have our thumbs in the ecological pie. We're crust and blueberries to the elbows. We control the amount of water flowing through a stream, the amount of forest given to a fire, the fertility of a field, the number of predator and prey species within a system. Everything within the ecological sphere shows the effects of our influence.

A Quiet Place of Violence

Continued control is necessary if only because of our previous disruptions. It is a question of lesser evils. Is it better to let a human-flawed system be harmed by suddenly withdrawing your hands or to alleviate the flaws through control and gradual stabilization?

There is also the unfortunate truth that the prairie dogs *are* eating the grass, which has a financial value for the rancher. For the New Yorker, it's an easy thing to let prairie dogs do—eat a little grass. But what if it's your cows, your livelihood, your kids' college education that's being eaten away?

According to a traditional social ethic where the process has been given no moral consideration at all, the rancher may completely exterminate the prairie dogs in order to have more grass for his cattle. But according to a process ethic, the rancher would have to maintain the population at a healthy level, even if it meant his own poverty.

It's a huge problem. Perhaps the largest problem.

When you come down to specific instances, the analogy of ethical rings seems flawed. Our obligation to the inner rings *does* change when a new ring comes into existence. According to the old ring, I can shoot as many gophers as I want, so far as I don't infringe on another's rights, but according to the new ring I have an obligation to manage the population toward the needs of the process. The social right and the process obligation, in this model, are mutually exclusive.

Which takes precedence, process or society? Personal interest or systems altruism?

It *is* the largest problem.

Within the span of a day, it has rained, snowed,

melted and gone clear. Now the frost and full moon give the trees a silver edge. Behind the trees, somewhere, a coyote howls. A hundred and fifty years ago this would have been a wolf, but wolves have faded into past tense so that we can stand in their place: predators replacing predators.

SPIRALS

A people can reflect their land, just as a land will, given time, come to reflect its people.

A local hired hand, aware of my attempts at game management and quite drunk, recently told me with a good-natured humor that he was going down into the Breaks to "kill sumpin'." Local stories are passed along at the dinner table, communicating essential information about regional identities. Two men were great friends until one reached across the table to steal a french fry and got his hand nailed to the table with a skinning knife. One time, Old Lou, drunk during a thaw in December, passed out in the mud and woke up with his hair froze into the ground. He knew that he was not well liked, and rather than let somebody get close to him with a knife, he had them piss on his hair until it thawed. The cowboy who owned the first car in the Breaks learned to drive by running it around in his corral. After he'd got the hang of it, he yelled out to his wife, standing by the gate, "Open 'er up!"

This is who we are, these stories say.

There is a curious coexistence, as in most remote areas west of the hundredth meridian, of a proud individualism with a fierce sense of community. The individualism is largely mythical, sponsored by an early diet of dime novels and film noir, but the sense of community is a geographical reality. Building, branding, and firefighting all need a neighbor's help if they're to be done with any efficiency.

This community protects itself through isolationism and libertarianism. Outside interference is bitterly resented. In a recent election between competing House Representatives, no one in Garfield County voted for the winning Democratic candidate. And when an environmental group proposed that 15,000 square miles of Garfield County and surrounding areas be turned into the "Big Open Great Plains Wildlife Range," the county responded by submitting that certain other areas of the country should be turned into parks as well—say, Chicago? The Freemen famously set up camp about fifteen miles from where I now sit.

In many ways, the Breaks provide an ideal for the conflict between society and process. "The Big Open" might be great for the environment, but it treats the ranchers and residents as inconsequential objects. It sees the process as the good to be protected, but it treats the people as a means to an end: This is, of course, abhorrent.

Process or society, which is more important?

A Quiet Place of Violence

Perhaps the series of circles is actually more of a spiral—a moral, hypothetical Fibonacci's series. Perhaps each apparent ring of the circle is connected to both the previous and the next. While I have an obligation to my family, I also have an obligation to my tribe, and my obligation to the tribe may impinge on my familial duties, just as my obligation to my family may impinge on the tribe. My sense of family may require that I have as many children as possible in order to give my children a support system, but my sense of tribe says that if there is a limited amount of resources for the tribe to exploit, I should have fewer children. Similarly, as the process is added to the spiral, I should have even fewer children, since the resources themselves are now found to have moral worth.

When Leopold says that we should strive to preserve the integrity, stability, and beauty of the biotic community, the assumption must be that this new set of duties will impinge on our old set—but not too much. We should strive to preserve the biotic community, so long as it doesn't interfere unreasonably in the preexisting sphere of society.

Of course, it's the unreasonable that's the catch.

Under this idea, it's not all right to appropriate the private lands of 1,589 individuals in order to benefit the environment, but it may be all right to impose financial sanctions on those people who don't recycle their tin cans.

In short, extremes of infraction into either side of the spiral are unacceptable if they threaten the basic integrity of that spiral.

If it is ethically permissible to strenuously punish murderers (since murder threatens the integrity of the social sphere), then it should be permissible to punish those who threaten the integrity of the process sphere. Intentionally clear-cutting vast tracts of land would be preventable through coercion, for instance, as would poisoning a raptor population to extinction. There is a basic point of solvency beyond which any system cannot recover, and this point must be defended.

But when coercion is used to protect the system, it must not be used in such a way that it impinges on the integrity of the social rotation. People must never be treated as a means to an end. If the essential health of the process is undermined by clear-cutting in the Brazilian rain forest, then it is probably permissible to prohibit it. But the obligation then arises to show the natives how to get by through selective cutting, or to provide them with a system of organic fertilization.

And this is the trick—managing to treat people as ends in themselves even while maintaining the integrity of the environment.

It would be socially unethical for the government to treat people as a means to an end, punishing those who have more than one child. Yet it's systemically sound for everyone to only have one child. Similarly, it would be socially unethical to force farmers to use sound ecological practices, yet such practices are becoming more and more necessary. It would be unethical to force an individual to hunt, usurping his other life's projects, yet hunting benefits the process.

The solution, as always with the ethics of intention, is awareness. It's the burden of knowledge. With the awareness of a felt need, a violation of the preexisting spheres would no longer be possible. If everyone realized the value of having only one child, then that is what everyone

A Quiet Place of Violence

would do. I have enough faith in humanity to propose this.

So should the rancher be prevented from killing gophers to benefit his cattle? All the gophers? Perhaps. Most of the gophers? No. Should he be made to see the benefits to the process in keeping a stable population of gophers on his land? Probably. Through awareness and experience, this newest ethical spiral gains solidity without threatening the premise of other spirals.

Nicely, the most intensely debated topic between animal rights lobbyists and the general population—medical experimentation—falls into this paradigm. Under a social ethic it is okay to use objectified animals to further society. But under a process ethic, medical research would be forbidden since it removes both the animals and the researchers from the system. However, when a social ethic is *moderated* by a process ethic, some experiments are permissible, the crucial ones. AIDS research would be allowable, as would research for cancer and diabetes, but the experiments dedicated to cosmetics would be anathema.

Ironically, at this end, we find Aristotle's doctrine of moderation once more appealing. We have come around far enough to recognize the validity of this past position, even while changing it slightly.

Spirals.

The tendency is for an ecosystem to expand rather than contract. It moves and it changes and it comes around to recognize itself in the line to the side, the line ahead.

Last year, hiking above Albuquerque, looking for cliff art, I was unsurprised to find among the dancing flute men and stiff-legged birds an intricate, finely-spaced coil.

A piece of earth art, Spiral Jetty, in the Great Salt Lake, 1,500 feet long and 15 feet wide, is meant to represent time, twisting away from the shore in a series of gracious circles that are never quite complete, containing within them nothing at all.

Even the stars perform on a helix, in a year never on precisely the same axis.

It is our anatomy, this; our cosmology.

Mind

*I*t's snowing, although it's really too cold to snow. What's in the air now is more of an icy mist swirling around the porch light.

I walk out to the truck wearing a heavy down coat, ski mask, mittens, binoculars, and a gun over my shoulder. It's supposed to warm up to ten degrees by midmorning, but for now it's well below zero.

The plastic seat cracks beneath me as I wait for the engine to warm. After a minute, I swing the truck around, illuminating the yard with the headlights, cutting and sharpening the familiar features: the log shed, the weedy farm equipment, the gate posts. This weather will almost certainly throw the deer into a fierce rut, but I won't give up the rifle until it breaks enough to make bow hunting reasonable.

I drive down the ridge to the mouth of Hay Coulee, to

where it opens out into the empty space of *Squaw Creek*, and park the truck on the highest, furthest point of the ridge. It's a good idea, especially when the light is flat like this, to put the truck where you can see it.

Ethics are useless if people are incapable of following them. You have to put your system where it can be used. Back when Genesis was being written, this wasn't a problem; God was the ultimate source of the ethic, and God was a badass. But now...

Existence precedes essence, Jean Paul Sartre wrote, and by the writing, became the first self proclaimed existentialist. Most of the other famous existential thinkers—Kierkegaard, Nietzsche, Dostoyevsky—have had the label imposed on them. But Sartre took it on himself. This is all there is, in front of us. There is no Platonic One behind it all. No pure ideal of snow behind this snow. No God to unite and give credence to all this corrupt phenomenality. This is it. Love it or leave it.

We owe him a debt.

But as important and perhaps as purging as existentialism has been, it still presents a problem for ethicists. How does one create an ethic when there is nothing beyond the real world, when, in fact, all things are relative to the observer? There is no good or evil in Sartre's world—we are all the final standards of goodness. It's a problem that Sartre himself was unable to solve, although he was working on it when he died.

By the time I've got spare shells in my pocket and the binoculars and rifle slung so they won't knock against each other, there's enough natural light to illuminate the bottom of the coulee. I start walking. The plan is to hike straight across the bottom, hunt the face of the other side, cross back over, and then work my way back down—a good half-day's circle.

Within a few minutes the mouth of my ski mask holds a crust of old breath, and my wrists, exposed by the swing of my arms, are briefly cold, then numb.

Up on the other side it feels warmer. There's even a little sweat under my arms. Large, heavy snowflakes begin to fall, and I tear off a piece of tissue to stuff over the lens of my scope.

Within ten minutes I can see my own, faint tracks in the new snow. Within twenty minutes these tracks have been filled in.

At the top of one of the ridges, I stand for a moment, catching my breath. The skin across my cheeks and nose is cold enough to have lost its elasticity.

I stare at a series of spots that could be deer but aren't, and then move on, glassing sporadically up and down the coulee for fifteen minutes or so. When it's apparent that nothing's going to show itself, I walk down the hill, across a small, terraced bowl at the head of the draw and up to a similar point on the next small ridge. Coyotes howl off to the north.

It stops snowing—not gradually but suddenly—and where a moment ago there had been only empty juniper and pine thickets, I can now sense breath and rustling.

Beyond existentialism's ethical problems, but related to them, there is a psychological dilemma. I am a thinking, reasoning, symbolic entity, a kind of God, yet I am going to die. This is an irreconcilable paradox—the "worm at the core" as William James called it—and it has screwed a lot of us up. We have attempted to deny it, and our denials have resulted in a variety of problems.

As small gods, we are also absolutely free. This is the commonality across all the various flavors of existentialism: the idea of freedom. We are free, and so we have no security or choice beyond our wills. My intelligence and rationality allow me to maintain an observing consciousness, an ability to stand back and say, "I can turn the television on or not," even if I know that in the next moment I will turn it on: thus, guilt.

But the process, it seems, would deny this freedom. While this is all there is, here in front of me, it is still enough to demand compliance. If I were fully within the process, I would have no choice of action at all. My actions would exist without intention.

Perhaps this is our final salvation from the absurdity found in existentialism.

Roderick Nash, in his now famous *Wilderness and the American Mind*, describes a 1972 psychological experiment in which fifty-one chronic mental patients (schizophrenics, sex offenders, etc.) spent a length of time in the wilderness. For over half of the "hopeless group," the experience marked the end of their hospitalization.

The coyotes have stopped calling. I drop down off this ridge. Halfway up the next, two does trot out from the pines, pause as they see me, and then continue their same path without changing speed. Snow lays across their wide, fat backs like saddles.

I pull the gun off my shoulder, expecting a buck to be pushing them from behind, but...nothing.

From the next point, I look down into a tangle of small drainages and pockets of timber. Scanning from right to left there is only landscape, but then from left to right, glancing back, a sudden elk watches me from a rise not two hundred yards away. He's a big six point, his scarred hide and gaunt ribs attesting to the recent rut. After a moment he drops off in a trot toward the bottom of the coulee, trailing tracks like punctuation.

The Christian era of domination is over. And perhaps existentialism is coming to an end as well. Perhaps we can find within the natural order a faceless theology, a religion to transcend questions of good or evil. This may be all there is, but it is enough.

There are practical benefits to realizing our inclusion within the process (game management and environmental stabilization), but perhaps the greatest benefits are to the individual him or herself. Existentialism tells us that we all feel ourselves to be the centers of our own universes. The great anxiety of life is in discovering our own staggering insignificance. The God that I had worshiped is no longer believable, and since he was what had convinced me of my importance, a new substitute must be found. A relationship to nature requires a loss of self and therefore a loss of the feeling of insignificance that comes with our sense of self. Hunt, and insignificance drops away like heavy wool.

I may be approaching these issues wrongly, but then, no one can be quite so emphatic as a Believer.

My fingers move sluggishly, not quite closing into a fist. When it's cold like this, the blood rushes to the internal organs and leaves the digits to suffer. It's a question of conserving what's important. Losing a finger or two won't keep me from reproducing, but losing a liver will.

It's snowing again, harder. The trees at the edge of the coulee drift across the horizon—pale afterimages of what they were an hour ago.

I shift and turn. A doe is walking up the ridge toward me, less than one hundred yards away. I watch her come. Another doe follows her up from behind, and then another, and another, until nearly a dozen does are visible through the trees.

Behind them, a pair of antlers grows from the back of the ridge. These pause, turn, and finally pull the buck up behind them. He's a good five point, with heavy antlers—but still no more than twenty-two or three inches. In most places he would be a very shootable buck, but here I can expect to get something better.

The does step lightly, delicately, with all their eyes fixed on me. The buck sniffs at one of the does, nudging her with his nose until she trots off to the side, and then he stops to stare at me too.

They are within thirty yards. Then twenty. I shift a leg…and that's all she wrote—the group scatters.

Alone, after you find your project to have disintegrated, you feel like a slide caught in a projector: suddenly, brilliantly, exposed.

From the next ridge, I can see the fence that I had planned on hunting up to and not beyond. I'll cross over from this ridge.

The snow dwindles away until the sun shines against it on the ground. The coyotes begin singing again, much closer. My feet are wet and I'm tired. I sit and pull out a peanut butter sandwich from my fanny pack.

A field of snow distills color, squeezing it out as if through a screen. The green of the pine tree in front of me, enhanced by small domes of white, is a pure green.

A Quiet Place of Violence

And its trunk, brown only yesterday, seems now tinged with red, like old flesh.

I stop chewing and stare. A doe is moving up the bottom of the coulee to my left, less than a half mile away. She stops to glance up toward me, but then continues on.

Behind her, there should be a buck...and there is. A good one. I move slowly, setting down the sandwich and picking up my binoculars. He's very good. He's about twenty-six, with a heavy pair of main beams and an extra point off the back forks on each side. This is the one.

I slide down onto my belly and rest the rifle over the fanny pack. Slowly, slowly, I slide a shell into the chamber. If they continue on their present course they'll pass right below me, less than two hundred yards away.

There's the well-known sense of waiting, of expectation, of forced stillness. I check my scope. It's collected a crack of frost. I scrape it away with my fingernail and look again. Fine.

They disappear into a patch of trees, the doe slogging along with the buck right behind her. In a few minutes they emerge on the other side, in range but moving closer. Through the scope, the buck's neck is swollen almost to his ears and he's licking his nose as he walks, sticking it out toward the doe. Oh, he's a good one. His antlers are dark and pure against the snow, his hide a distilled gray and white. He's beautiful. He passes directly below me, traveling at a good trot. I whistle softly, and when he doesn't stop I whistle a bit louder. That does it. He freezes and stares precisely up at me. In the few tense seconds I can feel him winding up, getting ready to jump away.

The crosshairs are on his shoulder, a little low since I'm shooting downhill, and I exhale slowly, squeezing off the shot. *If you pull the trigger you've already missed.* He *humps and kicks out his back legs and turns to run back down the hill. In less than fifty yards he falls and slides, coming to rest against the bottom of an eroded bank.*

The familiar emotions collect and build, layering themselves like dust, like a rolling ball of gumbo.

I run down the hill, sliding through the loose clay. Each step carries me ten feet in an avalanche of soil and snow. Halfway down I realize I've left my pack up on the hill, but I have my knife, which is enough for now.

His antlers are even heavier than I had thought, gnarled and twisted at their bases, but I don't think he's quite as wide. When I check his teeth, I find them to be worn and broken: an old buck. His body seems small, and this makes his antlers look bigger. He's not over twenty-five inches, and may not even be that—but it doesn't matter. I had thought he was, and this is the crucial point. It's always a greater temptation to shoot a buck after a hard hunt, when the process is behind the hunt, not simply the project.

His rut fills the air. I touch his eye to make sure that he's completely dead.

He's so fat. In turning him over to get at his stomach, the skin feels loose over the layers of it, and before I'm done gutting him, my hands are oily, and the locking mechanism of my knife is clogged with grease.

He's wonderful. Beautiful.

I climb back up to get my pack, the sudden absence of adrenaline making it laborious. Back down, I work to bone out the deer and put him on the pack. This is going to be a heavy load: antlers (but no cape), straps, loins, hams, and the meat from one front shoulder.

I do not have the courage, or audacity, to advocate a physical return to a hunting and gathering existence, to give up our colleges and cars in favor of wattle huts and stone spears. I find this idea vaguely ridiculous. But perhaps we should look into the possibility of a spiritual return, an embracement of the mind and soul that was the by-product of our original hunting and gathering existence.

The trick will be to learn how to distance ourselves from the ethic of separation even while retaining the necessary social fruits of that ethic. We rode the concrete, existential leviathan from there to here, but now we gotta find a way to send it back across the river.

I am a hunter, and all other features of my life submit to this fact.

Hunting is not a state of life but a state of mind.

I begin walking back to the truck, carrying a pack that feels like it could weigh eighty pounds. I'll follow the drainage down rather than hiking up over the ridges—but still it won't be a cinch. I'm already wet and tired.

After another couple of hours, sitting in the truck, I rest my hands on the top of the steering wheel, my head on the back of my hands. I shiver, my sweaty T-shirt catching the air from the heater. Icicles on my mustache and beard drip onto my arms.

This is the end of it. The end of the season. I'll be scouting for the friends and family who are coming to hunt the last week of the season, but for me this is the end.

Part III

The Paradox of Order

As humans, we have tried to impose order on a perfectly ordered universe, thus producing disorder.

We have approached the world with preconceived views, and if we have seen the world as disordered, it's only because we've been unable to reconcile it with our preconceptions, with our projects. If I'm a farmer, an untilled field is an insult.

The world has seen two principal orders, two patterns into which blocks are made to fit: the social and the natural. The social is our own, imposed by our momentary, small-godlike intrusion. The natural has stood away from us, usually against us. Cars and homes, schools and railroads, all have been created to facilitate a social order, not a natural one.

Attempts to disturb our social orders have brought drastic, often violent responses. At the turn of the seventeenth century, Giordana Bruno was burned at the stake for his idea that the earth rotated around the sun. We fought and died in Korea and Vietnam for the idea that capitalism is better than communism. After the first performance of Stravinsky's *Rite of Spring*—a pounding, disturbing piece—there were riots in the streets of Paris. When Cézanne began lengthening his arms and distorting his bowls of fruit, friends expressed concern for his sanity.

Inevitably, however, we become aware of the marbles we're walking on when a project collapses under its own, natural weight. A good earthquake, lightning fire, or flood can reduce any life to redundancy. To the extent that our projects conflict with the natural order, they *will* be overturned by that order. I'm farming, and have drained a series of wetlands, but these wetlands had helped absorb floodwaters. Should it surprise me when my fields are destroyed a couple of years later in an unnaturally powerful flood? I cut sharply into a hillside to make room for my house, creating a terrestrial form that conflicts with the process, and a slip puts my house in the creek the next spring. I'm a writer, and I write with an image of the books I will complete, but I'm dead before I'm half done. Death, the most natural event in the world, conflicts with *every* project—except one.

Consider the time, effort, and expense we devote to merely staving off, for a moment, the *natural* disintegration of our projects: changing the oil in the car, painting the house, jogging around the block. Most of our projects conflict with the natural order. Even if we have a sense for the way things should be arranged in the world, there will always be a larger order, a *natural* order, that precedes us. We see the world as disordered if we can't use it, but its use depends upon our own, imposed order.

Nearly all our projects are going to conflict with the natural world, if only in their absurd futility, their false sense of importance, gravity, and urgency in the face of our upcoming deaths. Only one project embraces death as the absolute that it is. Only one project confronts the absurdity by its very nature.

The antihunters have imposed a false order on their lives based on a misconceived perception of the world. Death is evil, they believe, and so the purveyor of death must also be evil.

But the world is its own, and it will have itself back.

It's early January, and heavy snows have been imposing a new order on the Breaks. A week ago, I followed a set of mountain lion tracks around a sandstone bluff, and yesterday I noticed how the deer have been feeding in the middle of the fields rather than on the edges.

This morning I've been invited to go ice fishing on Fort Peck Lake.

Deep snow increases the potential disintegration of my own personal orders. It can make a clunking universal joint or a thin stretch of ice lethal. The road down into Ghost Creek, the last half mile of it, is steeper than most staircases, making it impassable after a rain or thaw. But a heavy snow makes it almost *impassable, and this is somehow worse. I'm sweating by the time I reach the boat landing.*

I follow the previous tracks out onto the ice, the lake stretching out for miles to each side, booming and cracking. It's an accepted thing to do—driving out onto the lake like this—but it has always struck me as remarkable.

I round a rocky outcropping, my inside wheels rising a bit with the natural bulge of ice, and drive into the recessed hand of Lost Creek. A small line of trucks already hugs the shore. Twenty or so residents of Garfield County stand out on the ice, occasionally turning their collective heads to glance toward their holes. In the middle of them, at least twenty feet away from the shore, a large fire burns. Fire on ice: another accepted, remarkable thing.

I park at the end of the line and carry my auger and box of sets out to an open stretch of ice, nodding and waving to the familiar faces. I stop at a spot where the water should be only six or seven feet deep and begin digging. The auger bites into the ice and I sweat as the digging gets stiff. Ice is water fixed into a structure, an order, yet for me to fish I have to create a speck of my own personal order. Tomorrow morning the ice will have refrozen.

Hole to hole, I unroll my lines, resting the sinkers on the bottom and dangling the hooks with their minnows about six inches above the sinkers. I lean the ten-inch lengths of board up against the small pile of ice shavings and rest a bobber on top. Ostensibly, this is walleye fishing, but you never know just what could turn up. Last year I caught an eighteen-pound northern pike. This is an older brand of fishing, Sunday afternoon fishing. The line tied to a board rather than your big toe.

On my way back around to the fire, I check my first sets, and use the toe of my boot to knock out fresh skins of ice.

The group stands quietly as I come up to them, hands in big coat pockets or held out to the fire. One of them says my name. I shake another's hand. Children run around behind me, giggling, then stop at their holes to check their lines.

Almost everyone around the fire is related. Clinton, to my left, a farmer and rancher with a hand too thick to be shaken with any confidence, is father to three of the girls. The oldest girl, Jody, is married to Kelly, son of the previous owner of our ranch, and they have two children of their own. Kelly grew up on our place, farming it and ranching it. Jody's the group's good luck charm, catching fish after everyone else has given up. To my right, Kelly is telling someone about the pike he caught here years ago.

Nature and society. Here, they manage to coexist. Almost everywhere else we have forced the second to precede the first.

As much as I admire these people, and like them, there is still something between us, or a lack of something. If friendship is the sharing of experiences, then perhaps experience is also friendship's factor of limitation. Everyone to my right and left, circling the fire, was born here. Most of these children now attend the same one-room schoolhouse up on the hill, will go on to high school in Jordan, and then will marry each other. Each of them has been shaped by the land in a way that's beyond me. Their scars are natural scars, pointing to nothing beyond Garfield County. If a finger has been lost, the machine that ate it is still sitting out in the field. If self-consciousness separates us from God and nature, it is experience that separates us from other humans.

Animal rights activists are laughed at here, alternately in disgust and incomprehension. The question is, "How could anyone even think like that?" The consensus is that they are simply ignorant—that they are curiosities of the city.

Behind me, one of Kelly's and Jody's kids gives a shout and pulls up a small walleye, ten or eleven inches

A Quiet Place of Violence

long, and dangles it up for his parents, grinning. After a moment, after inspecting it again himself, he pushes a finger through its gills, unhooks it, and tosses it back toward the fire. On the ice, it freezes midflop. Kelly sets it beside the cooler to be cleaned later.

Children so often offer the most accurate insight into a culture, exhibiting with no inhibition the deepest and most enduring traits of their society. Unsurprisingly, the health in the Breaks is seen most clearly in its newest members. These are not simply children, as one local poet has pointed out, but men and women in training. The little boy tossing a fish out onto the ice to die and be eaten is not cruel, nor simple, but in the process of growing into an accepted wisdom. And it's a wisdom that has gained value only in the face of a larger, newer ignorance.

To be afraid of death seems reasonable, but to attempt to change it is ridiculous. While a child may accept the frozen fish as the way things are, the activist can't help but see some part of himself in the dying fish. Why else attempt to resist it? Why else, but to deny our own, inevitable disintegrations.

How would you like to be beaten to death with a club? Those white seals, with their big eyes? How would you like to be shot just as you walked over a line in Yellowstone? Those buffalo, those American symbols? In a culture still basically romantic, where emotions are cultivated and indulged over reason, most never get past this first burst of sympathy, this first rejection of what's shaggy and smelly in our own closets.

What a joke this is, this thing we're experiencing that we call *life*. To die is not the curse. To be aware of our deaths and *then* die, that's the curse. Awareness is the curse. Siddhartha said that all evil arises from the individual will to live—not a will to die, but a will to live. If we could accept our deaths as the inevitable facts that they are then we would find no reason for struggling, no reason for the perversions of life that these struggles imply. Pick any of the seven deadly sins, pride to avarice, study it, and find that its existence depends upon the resistance of our own, inevitable disintegration. We are all going to die, so what possible reason could there be for pride? We are all going to die, so what possible reason could there be for wanting more money, more things?

Gary Snyder begins a poem with a quote from an eastern mystic: "One should not talk to a skilled hunter about what is forbidden by the Buddha."

It's revealing that across the widely-varying spheres of animal rights activism, the arguments have in common a dependency upon human analogies. Peter Singer, one of the principal academic defenders of animal rights, has asked why, if it is all right to put an unwanted dog to sleep, it is not all right to put an unwanted street bum to sleep. Wayne Pacelle, the director of *The Fund for Animals*, typically draws a parallel between nineteenth-century American slavery and the twentieth-century enslavement of animals. Human slavery used to be just as accepted, he says, as animal slavery is today, so shouldn't we try to liberate animals in the same way that the African Americans were liberated?

First and foremost, human metaphors are inapplicable to the natural world, on any level. We have the ability to create our own order, our social order, and this is an order that places us against (if only momentarily beyond) nature. Social necessity and natural necessity march to radically different drummers. Slavery isn't a good analogy for our current treatment of animals given that it speaks to the social order, which is *imposed* and therefore changeable. But the natural order has been imposed on *us*, and is unchangeable. The Breaks deer will always die to be eaten, just as those that eat them will die, in an eternally regenerative, self-maintaining cycle.

I find it offensive that anyone would presume to condemn this cycle. It has produced, along with the rest of the world, the person who condemns it. Who *are* these people? If nature is seen as a good, then killing and death must be accepted as an essential part of it. Why is this hard to see? Why are even a few intelligent, respected people so passionately against hunting?

Here's the thing: Anyone who hasn't been enculturated into it, who hasn't been taught it, stands at a disadvantage. While hunting does perpetuate itself, antihunting breeds with a greater strength. It has society on its side.

Somewhere in *Life's Little Instruction Book* is this piece of advice: Don't try to prove your manhood by shooting defenseless animals. In *Jurassic Park*, the meat eaters are villainous while the leaf eaters are heroic. "Veggie?" The little girl says, reaching out to pet a brachiosaurus. A bumper sticker driving around in Missoula has a pair of bears taking photographs of a dead hunter over the caption, "The right to arm bears."

The antihunters are mostly well-intentioned. They are acting altruistically for a larger cause, and to this extent should be commended. Unfortunately, their cause is misconceived. They are not loving the animals as members of the process, nor are they loving them as projects within the process—they are seeing them only as objects, as ideas. They are dominated by sympathy without having had this sympathy tempered by the corollaries of the hunt and the kill. As a hunter, I am an extension of the animal through the process, and through my project the animal is an extension of me. Without the hunt, I have been separated from the animal, and can feel only impotent sympathy. It's a conflict of orders.

We have been displaced from the wilderness into a concrete vacuum of hair salons and geometric cemeteries. The antis must assume that the animals they are protecting want to be displaced as well. This, while the hunter is saying, "Bring me into *your* world."

Curious. Complicated. I'm projecting, of course, my own thoughts and feelings on the antis, but it's a huge problem: how to understand each other.

It has been remarked (and remarked upon) that the current attack upon hunting is part of a larger rejection of things natural, and that after all other original things in the world have been disposed of, hunting will fall as well.

And then, presumably, God will clap his hands over this crippled clockwork and be done with us all.

I glance back to my small cluster of holes and miss one of the perched bobbers. Ah. Close up, the skin of ice over the hole has cracked, showing that indeed the line has been pulled down. The bobber rests under the edge of the hole, and as I watch, it wiggles. I grab the board and begin pulling and winding up the line, feeling resistance only after a couple of feet. It's really too cold for the fish to be very active. Finally, a sauger comes twisting up through the hole, similar to a walleye except for its lighter coloration and smaller size. This one is a good three or four pounds. I unhook it and carry it back to the fire amid complacent congratulations.

A Quiet Place of Violence

Any definition of nature that excludes hunting reduces nature to static scenery and frozen animals. Either we are animals, and hunting can be justified by this animality, or we are *not* animals and do not belong to the natural world at all and the whole debate is reduced to nonsense.

For no other reason than it's about time, the fish start biting. Having already had my luck, my bobbers stay put. Everyone else around the fire runs to their holes, laughing and suddenly chatty. Jody, true to her reputation, has two sets bobbing at once. I reach down to the pile of old timbers and toss one into the fire. It catches immediately and begins, before my eyes, to disintegrate, the energy caught within it trailing away into open air.

I was talking about orders.

Peter Singer has gone to elaborate lengths to demonstrate the inherent value of individual animals and the moral questionability of eating them, experimenting on them, and euthanizing them. He does so primarily on a negative framework, demonstrating how all definitions that would give any kind of exclusive right to humans fail. He shaves away human ego by showing how we are not the only conscious animals, how we cannot be said to be ends in ourselves if animals are means, and how the Christian ideas of an exclusively human soul and God-given dominion over animals are weak. In other words, he balloons our social order to encompass members of the natural order. We should treat animals as humans, he believes, because…why not?

Within the framework of society, Singer's ideas hold value, and he may be onto something. The trick, however, is to refuse to enter into the discussion on these terms. We must first recognize that although the social order might be expanded to include animals, it would be much better to expand ourselves, our own minds, into the natural order. It is a way of conforming to the order that produced us, rather than forcing the world into an order that only we find appealing.

Not that this is a free lunch. An expansion of ourselves is also a movement away from our social egos. If we were ever to completely belong to the order, we would have no greater value than any other member. Coyotes, deer, trees, and grass would all have precisely the same worth as humans; each would have an equal role to play in the order. Individual value, if value could be said to exist at this level at all, is found only in the role. That which has no role in the order, a coyote in a concrete pen, a professor in a paneled cubicle, has no value. If I am hunting, then I have entered into a moral dialectic in which it is as equally permissible for me to be hunted and eaten (by a polar bear or lion, say) as to hunt and eat.

Within this larger order, life, any life, holds no sacredness to precede the sanctity of nature.

It is true that no human life is worth more than the next. But it is also true that all human life is dependent upon the process, and cannot hold a greater value than this process.

This is the chasm between the social and the natural.

And this is the final burden of the ethical spiral. A new rotation forces *everything* to be reassessed. Hunting is not a hobby. Or a sport. Or something to be done for free meat. It is an obligation. The individuals who follow hunters around banging pots should be made to spend a month in the Bob Marshall with only a rifle, skinning knife, and matches.

A Quiet Place of Violence

I have caught no more fish, but am satisfied. I shake hands around, pull up my sets, and walk back to the truck. From the edge of the lake, looking toward the fire, they seem a single, multi-jointed ring, these people of Garfield County, the parts of them calloused together.

I have a ranch in the Missouri Breaks. But it does not have me.

I drive back in my own tracks, the last to come and the first to leave. I'll broil my sauger and eat it trying to stare out of a black window. After supper, I'll step outside and name the winter stars. Orion is coming around again, Orion the hunter.

A mile or so before reaching the cabin, I see a pair of predator tracks traveling beside the road, heading straight through. From the next hill, I spot a bobcat standing in a fringe of timber fifty yards away. It has paused, one leg up, but as I watch, it drops to its stomach and hunches down into itself, chin and whiskers clogged by the blood of something small. As it turns to me, it licks around this red fringe, leveling its face of compounded wisdom down onto my own. Despite the windshield between us, I am caught. Grace and violence, beauty and blood. It tenses through its back and shoulders, breathes itself into a greater charge, and without intention, without noise or movement, disappears into the timber.

I drive on, having just seen everything that needs to be seen.

Paul Shepard gives us a word from the Greeks, sophrosyne, *which he defines as* "the skill of mortality." *To know death not as an intellectual exercise but as an aspect of consciousness, exposing you to the teeth of the world, this is* sophrosyne. *It is anguish at the sight of a* road-killed rabbit, it is joy at the sight of a bobcat rimmed in blood; it is a struggle to rejoin Heidegger's fourfold: earth and sky, gods and mortals.

We might, like John of the Mountains, turn away from such skills, eating bread and water among the peaks rather than the flesh of the world; we might, like St. Francis, argue that all of God's creatures have a right to exist as a part of God's family. Or we might beat death and life together, heart against soul, emerging amalgamated, tempered, having forgone our wish to live. Siva the destructor embraces Brahma the creator and Vishnu the preserver as night perishes into day, the bobcat eats his rabbit, and the stars dance to an eternal drum. Let the awe show.

Nothing has a right to its own life. The Breaks will have us back: the deer I shot, the elk I killed. The Breaks gives, the Breaks takes away. The best hunters know this, having given up to the Breaks all claims to their own lives.

We must catch grace where we may. I once had a ranch in the Missouri Breaks. But then I stood in a noiseless, motionless wind and saw a thing: possession is as possession does. And so I will have the Breaks back only when I have become a short, moveable feast. My greatest grandchildren will eat an elk that ate the grass that was grown with strands of my carbon.

For now, however, I am here only at my convenience.

The Breaks have their demands. They demand compliance. They demand a loss of self. They demand our very bones. Their lips are bloody with their demands. To live in the Breaks without blood is to deny them their due, and if we have sinned, it has been in keeping blood from them; or perhaps, in keeping it from ourselves.

Convenience is our sin.

Karen Kenyon

Allen Morris Jones is a book editor (The Lyons Press), a novelist (*Last Year's River*, Houghton Mifflin), and the author of more than one hundred published short stories, articles, essays, and poems. He lives with his wife and young son in Montana.

CPSIA information can be obtained
at www.ICGtesting.com
Printed in the USA
BVOW11s0613290916
463590BV00001B/29/P